where

thinking

and learning

meet

lane clark

Hawker Brownlow
EDUCATION

dedication

This book is dedicated to my precious niece, Delane. As a five year old, just beginning her academic journey, she reminds me of the critical importance of preparing learners for their future and NOT our past.

Published in Australia by

Hawker Brownlow
EDUCATION

P.O. Box 580, Moorabbin, Victoria 3189, Australia
Phone: (03) 8558 2444 Fax: (03) 8558 2400
Toll Free Ph: 1800 334 603 Fax: 1800 150 445
Website: www.hbe.com.au
Email: orders@hbe.com.au

Code: HB3522
ISBN: 9 781741 703528
0109

© 2009 Hawker Brownlow Education

Printed in Australia

ST VINCENTS
R.C. PRIMARY SCHOOL
VAUXHALL GROVE
BIRMINGHAM
B7 4HP

table of contents

about the author

Lane Clark has been examining the connection between real thinking, real learning and real assessment for more than 15 years. From this investigation, Lane has developed a comprehensive approach to teaching that seamlessly infuses these three vital areas into everyday classroom teaching.

Lane's public workshops and seminars have been very well received in Australia, New Zealand, England, Wales, Sweden, Canada and the United States. She has keynoted at national and international conferences on thinking and learning, and presented for a wide variety of Principals' and Deputy Principals' Associations.

Lane's range of thinking and learning classroom resources, including the *thinkbox* and *thinktower* thinking frameworks, the *think!nQ* learning framework; as well as a variety of 'real thinking' tools and processes, are used in classrooms by teachers and learners internationally.

She has written and published a 120 page *!nQuiry* resource kit and accompanying handbook titled 'Brain Basics' that is used in hundreds of classrooms around the world, and a multi-module 'home-study' course for teachers on thinking, learning and assessment.

Lane has developed the 'Get Connected' section of her website www.laneclark.ca, to offer past workshop participants the opportunity to engage in a unique learning community online. Although this community has only recently been developed, hundreds of educators internationally are now 'connected'.

She has been invited to present her ideas at universities, influencing the thinking and practice of the next generation of teachers, and her work is studied by education students in a number of Australian and New Zealand universities.

Lane has had a significant impact on the infusion of real thinking, real learning and real assessment into classrooms. Her thinking and learning tools, strategies and processes have been adopted by infant, primary, secondary and tertiary schools worldwide.

This is Lane's first book, but two others are expected to be released by Hawker Brownlow publishing over the next year; 'It's Bigger Than Criteria - Real Assessement' and 'Where Thinking and Learning Meet - A Companion Book of Thinking Tools'.

acknowledgements

This book has been a long time in the making and could never have been completed without the support of so many.

The greatest of thanks go to Ed, my business partner, and life partner, who initiated the early thoughts of this book back in December 1999 with the gift of a dictaphone and a journal inscription that read, '… well, get on with it then'. Your perfect balance of support and challenge drive me to become the best that I can be. To my father and brother, whose unwavering love, belief and support enabled me to take the risks and make the decisions needed to see my early professional dreams realised. Your continued love and support make a real difference in my life. So much of what I have done and continue to do is because of you both. To my mentor and friend, Gerry Smith, founding principal of River Oaks Public School in Oakville, Ontario. Thank you for teaching me, through your example, to dream my dream for kids and then make it happen. To my Teacher's College professors, Carol Howitt and Milree Latimer, whose words, 'teacher as reflective practitioner' have never left me. As promised, I believe that those words help me daily to become the best educator that I can be. To Barb Irving, founding director and leading teacher of the Discovery Centre of Halton, who introduced me to the concept of teaching children how to think and how to learn. To watch you work with children; and to watch them respond to the environment created and the learning strategies used, was truly a teacher-changing experience and one that will never be forgotten. To Donna Hall Clark, former Director of Staff Development, West Seneca School District, New York State. It was you who first invited me to share my work with other professionals. You believed in me then, and have continued to believe in, encourage and support all that I do. Thank you so very much. To Don Tinkler, a more recent mentor and dear friend, who challenges, supports, directs and redirects me as I continue on my personal learning journey. You exemplify the role of 'facilitator of learning'. I am grateful to you for both your guidance and friendship. To Kirk Mosna, my dear friend and graphic designer. There are really no words to thank you for your creative talent, tenacity, patience, feedback and friendship. I feel truly blessed to have you in my life. To Elaine Brownlow, of Hawker Brownlow Publishing, whose leadership, professionalism and vision inspire me. Thank you so very much for your guidance, support and patience! To Thea, Stephen and especially Carmen at Hawker Brownlow Education. You have worked tirelessly on the editing and design of this manuscript. I offer each one of you a heartfelt and sincere thank you. To the many amazing educators with whom I have had the great privilege of working. You have taught me so very much and have had such an impact on both my thinking and learning. Finally, and most importantly, I thank the children that I have been so fortunate to work with directly and indirectly over the years. You remind me not only of the incredible privilege it is to be a part of this profession; but also, of the great responsibility that I have to prepare you for your future, NOT our past.

preface

Literacy, numeracy, information communication technologies, learning styles, multiple intelligences theory, student criterion-based assessment, portfolio assessment, co-operative group learning, thinking tools, boy's education, indigenous education, gifted education ... I could go on and on. As an education system, we continue to send teachers to a diversity of disparate professional training opportunities and wonder, upon their return, why little has changed with respect to their overall practice. Perhaps the whole is greater than the sum of its parts.

Many years ago I set out to find the 'whole' and with that, an authentic way to seamlessly infuse all of the parts I was responsible to address with my learners. This book will share both my journey and findings, in an effort to offer an alternative perspective to how teaching and learning can look and sound in our schools, office buildings and homes. Because the whole is about teaching, learning and thinking, it transcends the classroom, age, ethnicity, gender, developmental level, context and purpose. As a result, this book is for anyone who has a vested interest in learning.

Consider what is involved in independent, self-directed autonomous learning ...

If an individual knew how to learn, they would need to make decisions, problem solve and effectively manage time; self assessment would be a natural part of the learning process as would outside assessment on occasion; the learner would need both independent and interdependent skills; and information communication technologies would be used effortlessly as the learner accessed information, recorded information and managed it. Technologies would be used to design ideas and of course to communicate both formally and informally. These technologies would be self-selected by the learner themselves. Some would be older technologies and others newer digital technologies. What is key here is that the learning dictates the technology decisions, the technology does not dictate the learning.

What about integration? This is yet another area of struggle within classrooms internationally. Interestingly, the only place that subjects actually exist are in schools. When a person learns in the real world, integration occurs naturally. In the development of a table cloth, cross-curricular knowledge and skills in the areas of maths, technology process, scientific knowledge, cultural knowledge, etc, would all be infused. Similarly, a garden design would necessitate knowledge and skills in maths, culture, science, geography, reading, writing, speaking and viewing, among a myriad of additional disciplines.

It is critical to recognise that there is a significant difference between 'theme' and authentic integration. Theme is contrived. Subject outcomes are pushed into a topic. At best connections are loose and generally not necessary. Conversely, integration, as described above, occurs when the cross-curricular outcomes addressed underpin the successful completion of a learning focus.

There is also the very new focus on thinking to consider. In some schools, states and/or countries, thinking has almost become a ninth subject. Real learning cannot occur without thinking. There is an inextricable link that exists between thinking and learning. While this relationship requires conscious attention, thinking is addressed naturally when the teaching focus shifts from *what to learn* to *how to learn*.

introduction:
the chicken or the egg?

What comes first, the chicken or the egg? Nowhere is this question more meaningful to me than within the context of learning and thinking. As discussed in the Preface, thinking and learning are inextricably linked. To try to address one, independent of the other, is to do an injustice to both.

Many teachers feel that their students' thinking is evidenced through their use of a Mind Map or 6 Thinking Hats tool. While these tools direct their thinking and perhaps enable them to think more effectively, their thinking will remain limited until the thinking tools are embedded into the thinking process, which in turn is embedded into the learning process.

Conversely, many teachers provide learners with an 'inquiry' process to 'teach them how to learn'. Upon closer examination, the approach provided is often little more than a research process. While it may lead to increased independence with respect to some skill sets, it generally falls short of promoting the development of deep knowledge, deep understanding, deep learning and far transfer. Until learners engage in an inquiry framework that truly mirrors the real life learning process and embeds the thinking process, learning will remain superficial and inauthentic.

It is the inter-relationship between the thinking process and learning process that will enable the learner to meet their true thinking and learning potential.

This book is organised into 4 sections:

Section 1: First steps to change
Because the approach outlined here represents a significant deviation from the ways in which thinking and learning are currently addressed in schools, I have chosen to begin our journey with a focus on change. Why is change so difficult? How can change be initiated? How can change be sustained?

Section 2: Real thinking
A deep understanding of thinking is necessary in order to fully understand the deconstruction of the learning process. As a result, I will examine the thinking process, thinking tools and introduce a thinking framework that will teach our learners how to think.

Section 3: Real learning
A focus on learning how to learn will follow. I will deconstruct the learning process and introduce the Clark *think!nQ real learning framework* as a model that mirrors the natural learning process.

Section 4: Where thinking and learning meet
Finally we will consider the complex inter-relationships that exist between the thinking process and learning process. In examining where thinking and learning meet, I will introduce a planning framework that will enable and empower users to design and deliver a comprehensive and authentic curriculum.

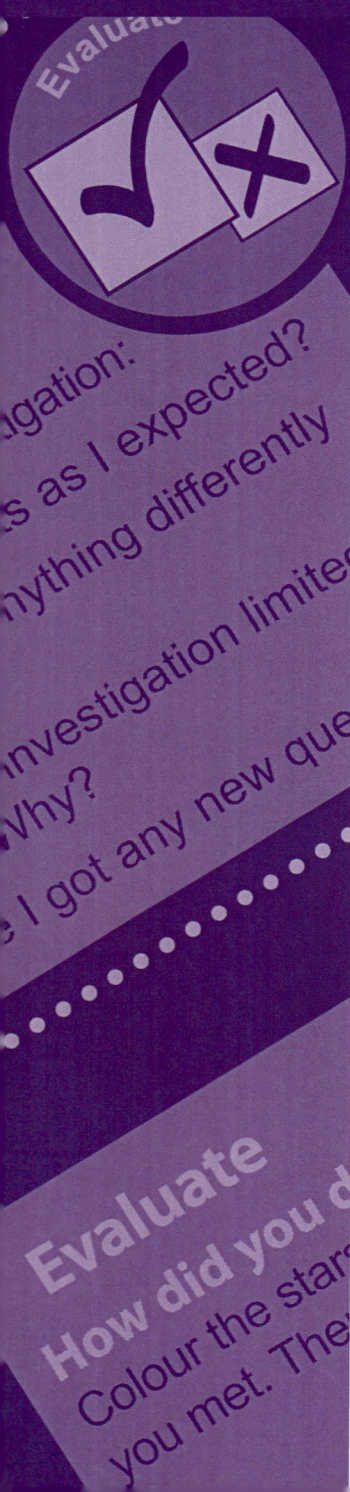

section one

Because the approach outlined here represents a significant deviation from the ways in which thinking and learning are currently addressed in schools, I have chosen to begin our journey with a focus on change. Why is change so difficult? How can change be initiated? How can change be sustained?

chapter one:
first steps to change

an overview of section one, chapter one: first steps to change

- Successful change comes from making your comfort zone uncomfortable

- Change doesn't come from looking at your strengths

- 'Real' beliefs are those that you talk and walk

- Your experience and reality guides your truth, your truth guides your beliefs, your beliefs guide your practice; if you want to change your practice, you must begin by challenging your experience and reality.

chapter one:
first steps to change

With best intentions and a sincere desire, we have all, at one time or another, set out on a change journey. All too often however, within a day, a week or a month, we revert back to old behaviours and practice. As I struggled to change my teaching and learning approach; as I left my comfort zone briefly, only to return, I realised that until I could work out how to change, I would likely continue this futile, albeit sincere, dance.

I set out to unlock the mystery of successful implementation and sustained change. I left my comfort zone, got 'out there' to trial new strategies and/or approaches. Eventually, the going got tough and when something had to give ... it was the new stuff. I returned to my comfort zone. It eventually occurred to me that what I needed to do was make my comfort zone uncomfortable! If I could make my comfort zone seriously uncomfortable, when I tried to return to that safe place, I would find myself more comfortable outside of it than I did within it. I didn't actually need to know how to change. If I could no longer return to my comfort zone, I would then stay outside of it until I found my way to change.

How then could I become uncomfortable with my current teaching and learning practice to the point where I could no longer accept my practice? I knew that discomfort would not come from looking at my strengths. I would need to consider my weaknesses. I realised that I would need to have more than a desire to change; I needed to have the desire to be honest, completely transparent, ask the hard questions and accept the not so pretty answers. I needed to challenge everything I represented as a teacher and learner.

It is important to acknowledge that, for some, this is no simple task. An individual must have strong self-esteem in order to challenge their core. I needed to recognise that I was a great educator even though some of my practices were less than great. I needed to identify everything I did well, celebrate those strengths and hold on to them. Still I needed to acknowledge that change would not come from looking at those strengths.

I decided to video my teaching. I put a camera in my room for a week. You see, I knew I could fake it for a day! I let that film roll and after a week's time, I viewed the video. I showed no-one but I was willing and able to look at it. I was I stunned at what I saw. It was painfully clear that, in many regards, I did not walk my talk.

I had always said that I believed that kids should be independent and self-directed. Then I watched the video.

Jeff had finished his work...

"Have you completed your learning journal?" I asked.

"Yes."

"Have you completed your homework?"

"Yes."

"Ah ... help Lisa," I replied hastily.

Now Jeff can't wait to finish his work tomorrow. Lisa is so helped, she is helpless.

My talk suggested a belief that students should be accountable and responsible.

Then I watched the video ...

When I wasn't developing the lesson plans, I was delivering them. I then marked my students' work; I wrote their report cards, and gave the parent an interview while the student was at home watching television. Now that's accountable and responsible! How could my walk and talk differ so significantly?

> *The important question is not what our schools will become, but what they might become. There is a critical difference ... The question of what will become implies the exercise of purely rational faculties, calling for trend analyses, projections, extrapolations and probability curves. A view of what could be is not confined to these means ... It embraces intuition, creativity, morality, reason and above all vision. It extends inquiry from the realm of the probable to the realm of the possible. Clear vision offers inventive, promising and powerful ideas for improving schools from within.*
>
> — Roland Barth, *Improving Schools From Within*

Our beliefs guide our practice. This I know to be true. You could come into my classroom, watch me teach and quite quickly identify my beliefs about teaching and learning. Similarly, you could visit a friend, watch him interact with his child and identify his parenting beliefs; visit a manager and identify his leadership beliefs. Having said this, individuals generally have two types of beliefs. Those that are espoused and those that are real. Real beliefs are those that you talk and walk. Espoused beliefs are those you merely talk but do not walk.

Real beliefs guide practice, but where do beliefs come from? For me, this was the critical question. I believe that beliefs come from truth and truth from experience/reality. If you have only ever known the teacher to design the lessons, deliver the lessons, mark the lessons, write the report and provide the interview, then this is your experience and your reality. Your truth would recognise these practices to be right and valid and this in turn would impact your belief system. Practically you would design the lessons, deliver the lessons, mark the lessons, write the report and provide the interview.

If your experience showed you that a five-year-old couldn't self assess using criteria, set personal goals, monitor goals and prove goals against evidence, your truth would concur. You would believe that they were not yet capable and your practice would reflect this.

So much of our reality and experiences as educators are shared. Because teachers go from school, to school, to stay in school, we share experience and as a result we share truth, beliefs and practices. It is difficult to challenge that which is collectively accepted and practised. When we share a mental model, we assume that what we are doing is right, and is best. For this reason education systemically looks very much the same regardless of school, region, state or country.

If I wanted to change I needed to identify my real beliefs but, as importantly, I needed to focus my attention on the experiences and reality that ultimately impacted my practice. I realised that I would need to identify my current reality/experience and consciously decide if it required challenge. Perhaps it wasn't right? Perhaps it wasn't best? Perhaps I did it because my teacher did it; and her teacher did it; and her teacher's teacher did it. I began to question the system. I began to challenge everything I did with my learners. Was I engaging in practices that were pedogogically sound? Were they best for kids? Were my practices reflective of real life learning and real life situations?

Children come to school around four or five years of age and learn in a classroom with others who share the same age and little or no experience in a formal school setting. At six years of age, now with one year of experience, students move along to another classroom. They share their learning with those the same age, now with two years experience. When, in the real world, have I ever worked with individuals who all share my age and number of years experience?

We invite learners to experience their classmates and their teacher for a one year period. At the end of that timeframe, students change classrooms; they are introduced to a new teacher; and a group of new classmates. Why? We know that learning requires risk taking, which requires trust, which requires relationship, which requires time. Just as our learners are getting to know one another and their teacher; just as the teacher is getting to know their students; just as relationships are developing along with trust; students are shifted into new classes, with new teachers and new classmates. In the real world I would never accept this practice. I would never wish to have a new boss and new colleagues yearly. Why do we do this to our kids?

Teachers write the report card for the parent. Why? It doesn't actually matter whether the teacher and the parent know where a child is, where they are going and how they will get there ... who needs to know this? Perhaps the report should be for the learner? This is not to say that the parent should not read it. But seriously, isn't a performance review in the real world developed for the employee, not the parent, spouse or sibling?

The teacher creates lessons and learning centres for their students. Why? When they leave school, who will develop their lesson plans and when will they learn through centres that others create? In the real world when we have something to find out we go to tools. I can find out by using a book in my library, or by accessing hundreds of books in libraries all over the world via the internet and the world wide web. I can use an encyclopedia to find out or access 5000 on a CD or DVD. I can talk with an expert face to face or I can phone, fax, email or connect via audio video conference. What is key is that I use tools to find out, not lesson plans and centres that my teacher designs for me.

We talk of technology as a tool and then we put the majority of our computer systems in a computer lab. Would I have a pencil lab that students go to once a week for 45 minutes and ever expect them to use a pencil as a tool? The tools that we use on demand are those which we have access to on demand. Perhaps we could have labs initially but develop a long term plan that phases the concept out. What is the succession plan where computer labs are concerned?

The more I questioned my experience and reality, the more uncomfortable I became. It wasn't long before my comfort zone became very uncomfortable. I was unsure of what I could change and I certainly had no idea how I would change. All I knew was that I had to change. And so the journey outside of my comfort zone began ...

You don't know what you don't know! Immerse yourself in new possibilities. What else could it look like? What else could it sound like? Professional reading, classroom and school visits, courses and workshops and most critically, reflection, can all promote challenge and offer new ways forward.

Action

1. Record your beliefs about teaching and learning

2. Video your practice for a minimum of one week

3. Review your video and record your actual beliefs
   (the talk that you walk)

4. Trace back the experience/reality that influenced the belief

5. Challenge the reality
   - Is this best for kids?
   - Is this authentic and reflective of the outside world?
   - Is the practice sound?
   - Am I doing what I am doing because I have
     always done it this way?
   - Am I doing what I am doing because everyone
     else is doing a similar thing?

Note: You don't know what you don't know! Immerse yourself in new possibilities. What else could it look like? What else could it sound like? Professional reading, classroom and school visits, courses and workshops can all promote challenge and offer new ways forward.

section two

A deep understanding of thinking is necessary in order to fully understand the deconstruction of the learning process.

an overview of section two, chapter one: thinking about thinking

- It's time to question the validity of Bloom's Taxonomy – what do you think?

- Thinking is not linear, it is not hierarchical, it does not occur in 'levels'; it is not promoted through a system of 'mastery'

- There are 'types' of thinking; one type is not higher or lower than another

- There are 'levels' of thinking within any one 'type' of thinking

- The *Clark real thinking process* demonstrates that all types of thinking are interconnected; and that there are levels within each thinking type

- The Clark *thinkchart* information organiser has been designed to embed the *real thinking process*

- The *thinkit* process is comprised of a sequence of organisers that enable and empower the learner to discover the characteristics of any concept or thing

- The *thinkitgreat* process takes the *thinkit* process further; the addition of one further step aids in the identification of 'great' characteristics

chapter one:
thinking about thinking

The term 'thinking tools' is often heard in classrooms today but how clearly is it understood? What are thinking tools and what purpose do they serve? How can they be incorporated into our practice? How should they be incorporated into our practice? How are they being incorporated into our practice?

Thinking, we do it all the time … we can't help but do it. It happens during maths class and it happens during recess. We certainly don't wait until 'thinking time' on Tuesday afternoon, and we don't wait until we are offered a tool to assist us. If thinking is so natural, then why do we struggle to describe it, understand it, intelligently discuss it and address it explicitly with our learners? Why is it such an ethereal phenomenon?

The difficulty may rest with the 'big push' but 'little support' we have been offered in the area of thinking. Apart from Bloom's Taxonomy very few frameworks have been provided to explain how thinking is developed. Very little has been suggested to challenge this widely accepted theory of thinking.

2001 Version
- **Synthesis**
- **Evaluation**
- Analysis
- Application
- Comprehension
- Knowledge

Consider Bloom's Taxonomy (Benjamin Bloom, 1956; revised Anderson and Krathwohl, 2001).

The Taxonomy of Educational Objectives was proposed in 1956 by Benjamin Bloom, an educational psychologist at the University of Chicago. Like other taxonomies, Bloom's is hierarchical in its design. Learning at the higher levels is dependent on the mastery of learning at the lower levels. The taxonomy therefore suggests levels of thinking in a particular hierarchical order; with each level of thinking dependent on the prior level. What do you think? Do you agree that knowledge represents the first level of thinking? Do you believe that evaluation is a higher order ability than idea generation or the development of a solution? *The Taxonomy of Educational Objectives* (Bloom, Mesia, Krathwohl, 1964) identifies skills representative of each level of thinking. For example, the skills of prediction, estimation, interpretation and explanation are outlined under 'comprehension' level thinking. The ability to compare and contrast is represented in the 'evaluation' level of thinking; and summarisation is noted as a skill indicative of 'synthesis' level thinking. What do you think? How many of us referencing Bloom's framework have taken the time to analyse and evaluate its contents, or its message about thinking?

In my opinion, discrepancy, inconsistency and confusion are pervasive in both the original framework and the revised edition. Still, Bloom's Taxonomy is readily referenced in education circles, curriculum documents and in education resources world-wide. Is it any wonder that educators are confused? What is your opinion of Bloom's Taxonomy … what do you think?

I find myself frustrated with the confusion, anxious with the time it seems to be taking to really move thinking into our classrooms, and excited at the possibilities that exist for making a difference in the lives of our kids. Let's do it … let's figure out this thinking thing; let's take away the mystique and let's change our practice … because we can!

If we are ever to develop our knowledge and understanding of thinking, we have to take the time, put in the effort and engage in conversations about thinking … we have got to think about thinking.

In addition to the questions asked earlier within the fabric of this text, the following questions may also be considered:

Thinking About Thinking...

- What does it mean to think?
- What are thinking skills?
- What are thinking tools?
- What is the relationship between thinking skills and thinking tools?
- What are levels of thinking? Do you believe that thinking occurs in levels?
- Is there higher and lower level/order thinking?
- What is the relationship between higher and lower thinking?
- Can you think at lower levels without higher levels? Can you think at higher levels without lower levels?
- What is the relationship between thinking and learning?
- Is it necessary to understand the relationship between thinking and learning in order to infuse thinking authentically into your classroom practice?

Bloom's Taxonomy and Real Thinking

Before introducing you to the specifics of my work, it might prove beneficial to first share my thoughts in the area of thinking.

As will be the case with many of you reading this right now, as a student in teacher's college I was offered Bloom's Taxonomy as 'the' definitive guide to developing an understanding of thinking. Further to this, I was advised to use this model to 'incorporate higher order thinking' into my lesson plans. And so I set out to decipher this model so that I could begin to design my 'thinking curriculum'.

Unfortunately or perhaps, in retrospect, fortunately, I struggled. The more I considered the model and what it represented, the more I found myself challenging it.

Original 1956 Version
- Evaluation
- Synthesis
- Analysis
- Application
- Comprehension
- Knowledge

"First there is knowledge and then comprehension, application follows, then analysis, synthesis and finally evaluation ... hmmm ... synthesis and then evaluation? Evaluation is the thinking associated with judging and deciding and synthesis thinking requires one to take the parts and put them together in a new and different whole. Synthesis thinking is generative and creative. Certainly the development of ideas requires a greater complexity of thinking than does the ability to make judgments. As an example, if I judge a story and outline the strengths and the weaknesses and then walk away, what have I accomplished? Surely the desired outcome would involve my ability to counter the weaknesses; identify recommendations for improvement or change. Evaluation must therefore be lower in the taxonomy than synthesis ..."

Clark changes, 1990
- **Synthesis**
- **Evaluation**
- Analysis
- Application
- Comprehension
- Knowledge

"... What about the rest of the sequence. Certainly you don't begin your thinking with knowing something and then understanding it? If I know I know it, I must have some degree of understanding or I wouldn't actually know it ... I may only know about it superficially, but surely I can't be considered to 'know' anything without some degree of understanding?

It was actually at this point that I began to challenge the accepted belief that thinking occurred in 'levels'. Instead, I decided that there were **types** of thinking, with **levels existing**

within each type. I knew that I could know and understand superficially or with great depth and breadth; I knew I could analyse at a lower or higher level; or evaluate at a higher or lower level. As a result, I implemented a further change to the Bloom's model.

Clark changes, 1990
• **Synthesis**
• **Evaluation**
• Analysis
• Application
• **Knowledge.Comprehension**

I was comfortable with my changes to the model thus far, but I was feeling uneasy about the ordinal placement of knowledge.comprehension in the thinking hierachy. Did it really belong first in the sequence?

"... You don't know what you don't know so you can't know what you have never heard of!" Before you know and understand anything, you need to **find out**. Certainly thinking begins with the finding out experience. The more solid this experience, the greater the opportunity for eventually knowing and understanding ..."

Perhaps the 'finding out' experience was intended to be implicit within Bloom's model. Recognising this possibilty, I felt it needed to be *explicit*. I wanted my learners to know how *critical* the 'finding out' experience was to thinking. If the 'finding out' experience is limited, thinking will be limited; if the 'finding out' experience is biased, thinking will be biased. I wanted my learners to know that the only way they take information into the brain is through their sensory organs - they see it, smell it, hear it, taste it, touch it. I wanted them to recognise the importance of a diverse, limitless, interactive and multisensory, 'finding out' experience in growing understanding and, ultimately, deep knowledge. Because of this critical aspect of thinking, I developed criteria to guide my students in their 'finding out'. They would need to access a minimum of four resources for finding out, and consider a minimum of two perspectives, in an effort to safeguard against a limited and/or biased experience; they would need to use most interactive/multisensory tools prior to more passive unisensory resources; and they would need to select their order of tool use to ensure they moved from strength to struggle. Once again, I made changes to the Bloom's model ...

Clark changes, 1990
• **Synthesis**
• **Evaluation**
• Analysis
• Application
• **Knowledge.Comprehension**
• **Information**

"OK ... so you engage in finding out (information thinking) and immediately you understand it and know it ... this seems to be a HUGE jump! How does one move from finding out new information to understanding it and truly knowing that information?"

I found it difficult to accept that this transition was implied, as if it actually occurred innately. The more I reflected on this challenge the more excited I became at the prospect of what this change in the model might mean for my teaching and learning.

Let's do it ... let's figure out this thinking thing; let's take away the mystique and let's change our practice ... because we can!

"It's **PROCESSING**! I take in new learning and begin to process it ... processing occurs immediately ... it occurs regardless of whether I am cognisant of it ... as I find out, I process innately. If I could 'unpack' what occurred when I processed, I could deliberately and strategically direct my learners in their processing and consequently impact their thinking and learning outcomes. So what occurs when I process? I examine what I am taking in; considering the parts of what I am being exposed to (that's analysis); I judge what I am taking in; do I agree or disagree with this new information? (that's evaluation); and I question or challenge the new information or my current understanding or foundation of knowledge (that's synthesis). This processing leads to a NEW understanding.

Clark changes, 1990
- **Synthesis**
- **Evaluation**
- Analysis
- Application
- **Knowledge.Comprehension**
- **PROCESSING**
- **Information**

As I deconstructed how thinking occurred, it became increasingly clear why I could no longer accept Bloom's Taxonomy in any form; neither the original nor revised edition. Bloom maintained that understanding must be achieved in order to successfully engage in analytical, evaluative and synthesis thinking. Contrary to this, my deconstruction demonstrated that without analysis, evaluation and synthesis (processing), understanding would NEVER be realised. Bloom also differentiated between comprehension and synthesis. In contrast, my analysis led me to the conclusion that synthesis can be defined as 'the parts in a new and different whole', and therefore that comprehension is synthesis. In short, if your understanding after processing is different to what it was prior to processing, then your understanding is NEW. Because synthesis represents the 'new' thinking, then understanding can be considered to be synthesis thinking at a *low level* or a near transfer!

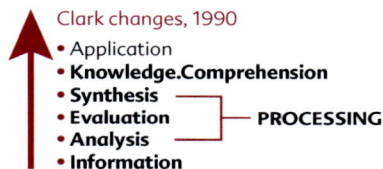

Clark changes, 1990
- Application
- **Knowledge.Comprehension**
- **Synthesis** ⎤
- **Evaluation** ⎬— **PROCESSING**
- **Analysis** ⎦
- **Information**

Bloom suggested that application could not be engaged in until a learner understands. I know, however, that if I apply I will understand better! Because application requires the use of multiple senses, processing is enhanced when one applies knowledge. I began to recognise the importance of early application in developing thinking. While it would likely be weak, ultimately, early application would result in an increased level of understanding. Subsequent attempts at application would become more effective and would further promote processing and depth of understanding.

As far as application was concerned, I began to see it on the synthesis continuum. Understanding grows. As one finds out, analyses and evaluates incoming information, questions develop, as well as a level of new understanding. With an increased level of understanding, new incoming information is again analysed and evaluated, and new understanding is further developed. As the process continues understanding becomes deeper and broader, the analysis, evaluation and synthesis associated with processing also becomes richer, and application of the new knowledge can result. Application results in further finding out, and the analysis and evaluation can eventually lead to the kind of deep knowledge and understanding that enables and empowers a person to be truly creative and generative: synthesis at a far transfer. As the result of my new 'thinking about thinking', it became overtly evident that Bloom's Taxonomy was significantly flawed. While all new ideas rest solely on the shoulders of giants, this giant's time had come to an end. I set out to construct a model that could be used by teachers and learners to develop their own understanding of thinking, and represent what I call the *Clark real thinking process*.

The *thinkbox* model appears on p. 12. The model will be dealt with in more detail in Section 3. Following this are a sequence of graphics to assist in my illustration of the *Clark real thinking process* as it relates to the design of *thinkbox*.

thinkbox

In examining the *thinkbox*, you will notice that the information and knowledge.comprehension (low level synthesis) form the base or foundation of thinking; analysis and evaluation occur side by side, as I believe this thinking occurs simultaneously; finally, as the pinnacle of thinking, high level synthesis is depicted. Contrary to a 'hierarchy', all thinking in the *Clark thinkbox model* is connected, as I believe this better illustrates the complex and interconnected reality of the thinking process. Rather than addressing thinking in levels, I will refer in Section 3 to **types of thinking** that are **inextricably linked**. We will later discuss the 'levels' of thinking within any one 'type' of thinking. For example, you can think at a higher or lower level of analysis; a higher or lower level of knowledge.comprehension.

We will detail the *Clark thinkbox* model, as well as its application, in Section 3 of this book. Before shifting our focus, you will find a sequence of graphics to assist in my demonstration of the *Clark real thinking process*, a conceptual framework that illustrates how depth and breadth of thinking are developed; and far transfer of learning achieved.

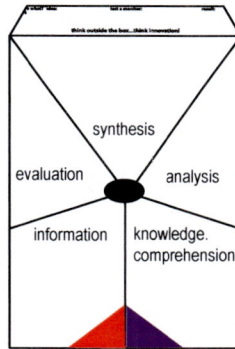

1. All learners come to new learning with some prior information, knowledge and understanding. They may not have much depth or breadth in this foundation, but they are not an empty 'box'.

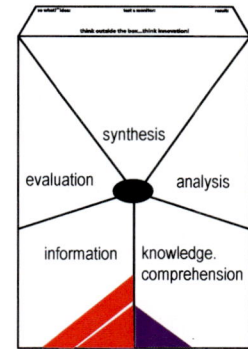

2. The 'finding out' experience begins. Learners take in information via their sensory organs. Five sensory resources are used first; a minimum of four tools are accessed; multiple perspectives are encouraged; learners select their order of use so that resources addressing modalities of strength are experienced before those which may prove more challenging.

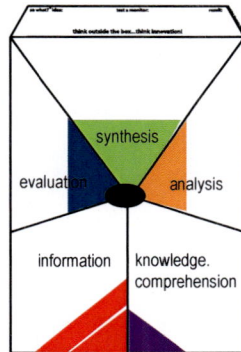

3. 'Internalisation' or processing begins, and learners analyse and evaluate newly accessed information; synthesis occurs as learners develop questions and/or challenge new information; while the learner must analyse, evaluate and synthesise in order to process new information, this early thinking is weak and superficial, lacking in depth and breadth.

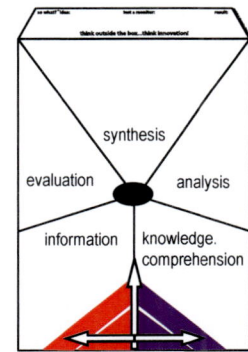

4. The processing of newly acquired information has led to the development of a broader and deeper foundation. Deep knowledge and understanding is becoming a reality.

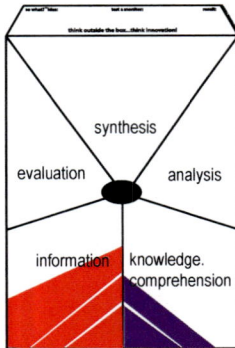

5. The 'finding out' experience continues ...

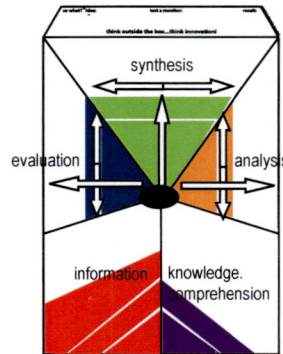

6. The learner processes the new information as they engage in analytical and evaluative thinking; questions become richer as the learner's foundation of knowledge deepens and broadens; and a new level of understanding is once again achieved. It should be noted that as the thinking process continues, so too does the learner's ability to analyse, evaluate and synthesise: depth and breadth is developing in each of these areas.

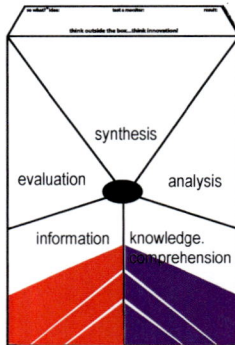

7. Knowledge and understanding continue to grow. As this foundation develops, the gaps between the information and knowledge.comprehension types of thinking and the analysis, evaluation and synthesis types of thinking, are decreased. While analytical and evaluative thinking occur naturally when processing, it is important to recognise that early analysis/evaluation type thinking is generally shallow and subsequently weak. As a foundation of thinking develops, the gap closes; subsequently, analytical, evaluative and synthesis thinking become anchored, more complex and much more rich.

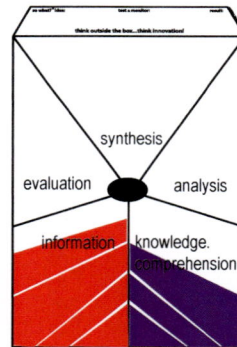

8. The 'finding out' experience continues ...

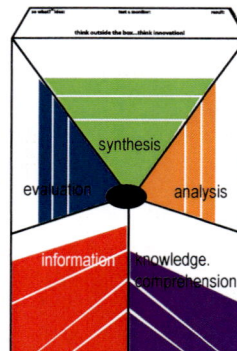

9. The processing continues ...

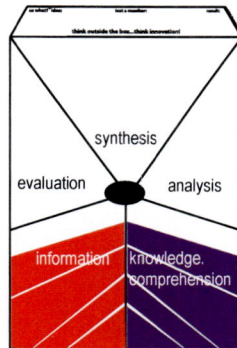

10. Knowledge and understanding continue to deepen and broaden ...

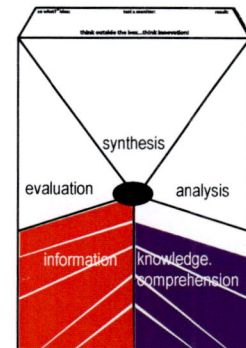

11. The 'finding out' experience continues ...

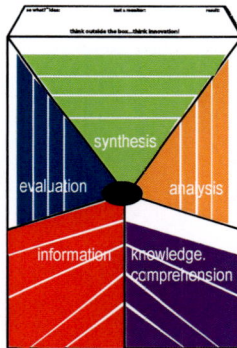

12. The processing continues...

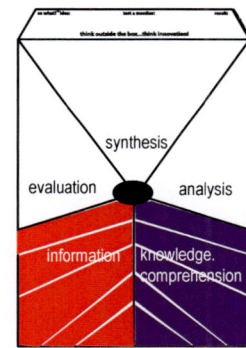

13. Curriculum internationally is aspiring toward the goal of 'deep knowledge and understanding'. All too often, writing teams neglect to instruct the teacher as to how this can be achieved. It is as if the mandate alone is enough! If the learner engages in a learning experience that enables the cyclical and adaptive process being described here to occur, a deep, broad and solid foundation of knowledge and understanding can develop. I believe that it is only through the thinking process outlined here that this desired outcome can be achieved.

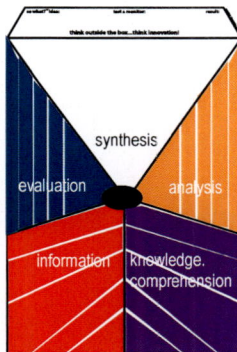

14. Deep knowledge and understanding has grown over time through a 'process of thinking' and learning. With this new foundation solidly in place, learners can engage in the *deep analysis* and the *deep evaluation* of new learning. This anchored thinking sets the learner up for high level synthesis or 'far transfer'.

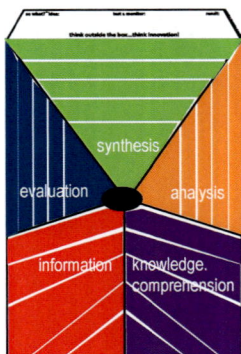

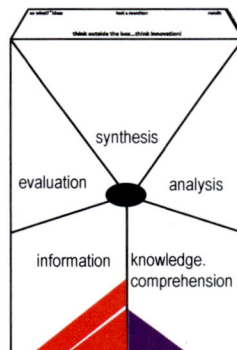

15. Learners can now consider their new learning and ask the question that I believe is the precursor to true creativity ...

"So I know it ... *so what*? I need to analyse and evaluate my learning and consider 'how can I USE my new knowledge and understanding to make a difference in my life and the lives of others?' Can I solve a problem I am now aware of? Can I develop alternatives or recommendations? Can I design a plan, a product or a vision? Can I use patterns and trends to predict the future?"

High level synthesis represents a far transfer!

Of course, the ability to develop questions is also representative of 'synthesis' type thinking. Limited knowledge and understanding will result in limited or superficial questions. As the foundation grows, so too does the richness of the questions posed. You see, "... you don't know what you don't know so how can you ask a question based on knowing very little?" Educators spend countless hours participating in in-service opportunities that focus on the development of questioning skills. It is remarkable to see how easily and authentically learners can develop questions when they have a foundation of knowledge to springboard from.

Regardless of the thoroughness of the thinking process engaged in, a learner can NEVER know and understand everything about an inquiry focus. This is represented by the gaps evident at the top of the information and knowledge.comprehension sections of *think-box*. While students will eventually be able to 'USE their learning to make a difference in their life or the lives of others', new questions will result in new inquiries and the process of learning and thinking is new again!

16. The 'finding out' experience begins again. Learners take in information via their senses.

Action

1. What are the implications of 'thinking as a cyclical and adaptive process on teaching and learning'?

2. What are the strengths and weaknesses of your current approach to developing your learners and teachers or employees as thinkers?

3. How are you currently promoting the development of deep knowledge and understanding, and ultimately far transfer, in your organisation or classroom?

putting the parts together

What, then, are the implications of the 'thinking process' on teaching and learning? I believe that we invite and expect learners to 'do it' too quickly. A learner's ability to 'create', 'invent', 'design' or 'produce' anything requires high level synthesis type thinking. This thinking, simply put, requires the learner to 'take the parts and put them together in a new and different whole'. All too often, however, students are expected to engage in learning representative of this type of thinking after being provided with little more than some research time, class discussion and a criteria sheet. If learners are to 'produce' quality, deep knowledge and deep understanding must be developed first. The development of deep knowledge and understanding necessitates the deliberate engagement in all other types of thinking, prior to idea generation and idea action. It is no wonder that many learners submit superficial, quality poor, creativity poor end products or 'endcomes'.

For example, let's consider how we might support our learners in their quest toward quality formal speaking. Skills required include the learner's ability to attend to volume, tone, pacing, body language and facial expressions. The learner would also need to consider the message being sent; the feelings they wished to evoke; and, of course, the purpose of the communication.

Before the learner can employ these skills effectively, they would have to identify each element individually. By deconstructing a diversity of formal speaking and presenting examples, the learner would be provided the opportunity to explicitly engage in this identification and thus establish a foundation to build upon.

Once a learner recognises the different elements that constitute formal speaking and presenting, the next step is to develop a deep understanding of each of these elements. This can be achieved through an explicit examination of each element. For example, 'Why did the speaker in example 1 speak so quickly, while the speaker in example 2 used slower pacing? How did each example of pacing impact me or the audience at large?' Engaging in analytical and evaluative thinking at this point in the learner's investigation will result in a deeper understanding of each element.

Comparing an element across a diversity of examples and then judging the specific usage of each element will further assist the learner in establishing depth of understanding. By determining the strengths and weaknesses of each deconstructed sample, the learner sets themselves up to generate personal ideas for quality speaking and presenting. Now the learner is ready and able to 'take the parts and put them together in a new and different whole … their new whole!'

Figures on pages 19—21 more accurately illustrate the thinking and learning journey required if teachers and learners are to recognise and be true to 'thinking as a process'…

thinking as a process

thinking to learn ...

Desired End
SYNTHESIS

Even the best criteria will not empower learners to produce quality. Deep knowledge and understanding must first be achieved.

Produce QUALITY
Formal Speaking/
Presenting
• volume
• tone
• pacing
• body language
• facial expression

INFORMATION

Find out about formal
Speaking and Presenting
• volume
• tone
• pacing
• body language
• facial expression

Learners are immersed in
positive/negative examples
of formal speaking

Experience is diverse,
multisensory, interactive
• newsreaders
• game show presenters
• award show presenters etc.

Experience includes diverse
technologies:
• email
• fax
• audio/video conferencing
• face to face interviews
• CD/DVD
• websites
• radio
• television

Learners must first be immersed in a diversity of speaking examples. They will use these examples to 'find out' about formal speaking. The more diverse, interactive and multisensory this experience, the better the chance a learner will have to take in the new learning so that they can process it.

thinking as a process

KNOWLEDGE. COMPREHENSION

Demonstrate basic/superficial understanding of the 'Elements of Formal Speaking'

Identify the elements in multiple samples
• purpose
• audience
• volume
• tone
• pacing
• body language
• facial expression

> By explicitly identifying elements in multiple examples, basic knowledge and understanding is demonstrated. The level of knowledge and understanding achieved at this early stage of the thinking process and learning process is generally superficial. Consequently an attempt to 'design', 'create' or 'produce' at this time would likely result in a superficial or low quality end product.

ANALYSIS

> By explicitly engaging learners in analytical thinking, processing is promoted and a deeper level of knowledge is achieved.

Begin the 'processing' required for the development of depth and breadth of understanding

Examine the elements identified in multiple samples
WHY - cause?
EFFECT - impact or result?

sample no. 1
• why did the speaker choose that volume?
• what was the impact on the audience?
• why that tone?
• impact on audience?
(examine remaining elements)

sample no. 2
• why did the speaker choose that volume?
• what was the impact on the audience?

thinking as a process

EVALUATION

Knowledge and understanding are deepened further as learners engage in explicit evaluative thinking.

Continue the 'processing' required for the development of depth and breadth of understanding

Judge the use of elements in each sample:
STRENGTHS
WEAKNESSES

sample #1
• what were the strengths and weaknesses of the speaker's volume?
• what were the strengths and weaknesses of the speaker's tone?

(judge remaining elements and subsequent samples)

Desired End
SYNTHESIS

The characteristics of formal speaking take on new meaning for the learner ... deeper meaning. Consequently, learners are enabled and empowered to design their own ideas for quality speaking and presenting.

Deeper knowledge/ understanding about the elements of formal speaking empowers and enables learners to design their own ideas for quality speaking and presenting

Produce ...
• Do it!
• Create!
• Develop!
• own ideas for formal speaking

tools to promote thinking as a process

If we want our learners to develop deep knowledge and deep understanding; to produce quality; and ultimately to be able to 'USE their learning to make a difference in their lives and the lives of others', we MUST engage them EXPLICITLY in the *Clark real thinking process*.

Processing will occur in spite of anything we do as teachers. Having said this, one difference between our 'gifted' learners and 'struggling' kids is their innate ability to process. 'Gifted' learners have the scaffolds in place to engage in this cycle of processing independent of outside intervention. The majority of learners do not. They process, but it is generally weak and superficial. As teachers, we have the ability to ensure that ALL learners process better.

We can engage them explicitly in the real thinking process and can offer them the **tools** to ensure that their thinking is directed and comprehensive.

It is also important to ensure that the process is repeated. Even if we invite our learners to find out and identify elements (information/knowledge.comprehension); examine (analyse); judge (evaluate); and challenge, question and generate their own ideas (synthesis), it is critical that this thinking be experienced and re-experienced. It is the cyclical and adaptive process of thinking that enables and empowers our learners. The delivery of curriculum must change to address this need.

Before I move on I would like to reiterate my last statement:

"As teachers we can provide our learners with tools to ensure that their thinking is directed and comprehensive."

There are many educators who intuitively or deliberately promote the processing of their learners by asking the right question, of the right student, at the right time. On the surface this may sound desirable. However, upon closer examination it becomes clear that the learner was dependent on the teacher to think. Given that different learners require different degrees of processing at different times, this reliance will prove challenging for the teacher trying to simultaneously cater to so many.

The *thinkchart* information organiser, the *thinkit* and *thinkitgreat process*, have been strategically designed to embed the *Clark real thinking process*. Use of these tools by your learners will result in the independent development of depth and breadth of knowledge and understanding; and their subsequent ability to achieve far transfer.

the *thinkchart* information organiser

Thinkchart is an information organiser strategically developed to embed the *Clark real thinking process* within its design. Use of the *thinkchart* results in the development of deep knowledge and deep understanding, and engages the user both cognitively and emotionally in their learning.

To ensure that rigour is maintained during student-led investigations, specific areas for exploration are outlined explicitly on the left side of the organiser. The elements selected and outlined in this area of the organiser directly correspond to the level of depth and breadth which will be achieved during the learning experience. Consequently, teachers and learners can manipulate these elements to meet the specific needs of individual students and curriculum outcomes. Student interest is recognised through the inclusion of 'blank sections'; learners are encouraged to self-select additional elements for investigation. To engage the learner cognitively and emotionally and to ensure the development of all types of thinking, *thinkchart* has been designed to include a number of further components along the top portion of the organiser.

thinkchart — investigating fairytales

Characteristics / Diversity	**P** physical	**B** cause (why) / effect (impact) behavioural	**E** setting / plot environmental	☺ strength	☹ weakness	✎ *so what* ideas
Beginning Words (once upon a time ...)		C E	•• •			
Victim (hurt)		C E	•• •			
Villain (baddy)		C E	•• •			
Hero (goody)		C E	•• •			
Problem		C E	•• •			
Resolution		C E	•• •			
Magic		C E	•• •			
Abuse		C E	•• •			
Ending Words (... happily ever after.)		C E	•• •			
		C E	•• •			
		C E	•• •			

thinkchart

The 'PBE' — Physical/Behavioural/Environmental Attributes = Characteristics

When collecting data, learners do not simply identify and record what they have 'found out' (physical attributes - P); they must also consider the cause and effect of what they have discovered (behavioural attributes - B); as well as the environment or location of what has been discovered (environmental attributes - E). This comprehensive approach to inquiry explicitly engages the learner in both analytical and evaluative thinking. Learners must often speculate, infer or hypothesise with regard to the 'cause' and 'effect' components. This not only engages learners in synthesis type thinking but often provides the springboard for student led *!nQuiry* as learners attempt to verify hypotheses or seek unknown answers. Consequently, the development of deep knowledge and deep understanding is encouraged as learners are explicitly directed to analyse, evaluate and synthesise new learning.

The *S.W.SW* — Strength/Weakness/*So What* Idea

The inclusion of *S.W.SW* (Strength.Weakness.*So What* Idea) section on the *thinkchart* further promotes the development of deep knowledge and understanding as it also infuses the *Clark real thinking process* in its design. Analytical and evaluative thinking are encouraged as learners consider the strengths (S) and weaknesses (W) associated with newly acquired knowledge. The inclusion of this SW (*so what* ideas), invites synthesis type thinking as learners are directed to counter identified weaknesses AND generate ideas for using their new knowledge. "So you know it ... *so what*? How can you USE what you know to make a difference in your life or the lives of others? Can you solve a problem you are now aware of? Can you generate alternatives ... new possibilities ... a new product?" This aspect of the tool directs learners to the *thinkbox* model where *so what* possibilities are explicitly identified. This will be addressed in greater detail in Section 3 of the book.

By promoting student led investigation that maintains rigour, student independence and teacher accountability become a reality. By engaging the learner to go beyond finding out and recording what has been researched, real thinking is developed and real learning is experienced. Learners are engaged both cognitively and emotionally, and learning becomes purposeful and relevant as learners eventually put their *so what* ideas into action!

Modifying the *thinkchart*

As with all organisers, *thinkchart* can be modified in an effort to reduce or increase complexity. In the example provided on page 25, the 'cause' component has been maintained, while the 'effect' component of the 'behavioural' section and the 'environmental' section have both been eliminated. The omission of these elements has minimised the rigour and thinking of this investigation. The learner is no longer considering the 'effect' of the arts element on the audience; further to this, an awareness of 'where' the element is found in the overall image is also omitted. In framing an organiser, the developer must recognise that what is or is not included will have a direct impact on what is explicitly discovered. Framing must be done consciously, with consideration to the endcomes that will or will not be achieved. In the 'fairytale' *thinkchart* the 'E' (environmental) section could be omitted in an effort to reduce complexity. Redesigning for simplicity in this regard could impede learning as the explicit relationship between story elements and plot would no longer be evident. Strategic design is key!

thinkchart — What are the characteristics of an artist's image?

Discoveries / Diversity	Dominance What is the first thing you see? cause WHY?	Colour What colours do you see? primary / secondary / tertiary / neutral cause WHY?	Line What kind of lines do you see? horizontal / diagonal / thick / vertical cause WHY?	Shape What kind of shapes do you see? rectangle / circle / triangle / square / polygon cause WHY?	Technique How did the artist work with the medium? • experiment with the technique and include sample • research actual technique applied cause WHY?	Feelings/Message What do you feel when you look at the work of art? What does the image 'say' to you? cause WHY?
name of piece?/artist — What do you see?					prediction / actual	feeling?
Why? OPV artist	WHY that dominance?	WHY those colours?	WHY those lines?	WHY those shapes?	WHY that technique?	message?
S 🙂						
W 🙁						
SW 💡						

thinkchart

SOSE *thinkchart* — What are the characteristics of environments at risk?

characteristics / diversity	physical what do you see?	cause - why?	behavioural	effect - impact - *C & S?* People, Animals, Plants, Environment, Global Planet P A PL E GP	environmental where is it found? • in your region • elsewhere in the world
geographical location	latitude - longitude - continent -				
Topography — above sea level •mountains (ranges, peaks, volcano, munatak, arete) • plateau •plains •rivers, glaciers					
below sea level •submarine landforms (seamounts, abyssal plains, canyons) •continental shelf					
liquid •oceans •currents •rain					
solid •ice shelves •glaciers •icebergs •snow •hail					
vapour •humidity					
atmosphere •troposphere (weather) •stratosphere (planes) •ionosphere (solar/ozone) •exosphere (outer space)					
Climate — temperature •daily minimum •daily maximum •average monthly •average annual					
precipitation •type (rain, hail, snow) •average monthly •average annual					
humidity •relative humidity					

©Ian Ayre, Graham Bailey, Lane Clark   * C & S consequences and sequels copyright Edward de Bono/*thinkchart* copyright Lane Clark

As indicated earlier, the *thinkchart* can be framed to increase the complexity of processing (and therefore thinking) required. In the example provided above, learners are directed to consider the immediate, short term and long term effect on a diversity of explicitly named elements (i.e. plant, animals, people etc). As a result, depth and breadth of knowledge and understanding are promoted through the strategic framing of the 'behavioural' section of this *thinkchart*. The *S.W.SW* component of the *thinkchart* attaches to the right side of the organiser at the dotted line.

thinkchart examples

In an effort to illustrate the flexibility of the *thinkchart* organiser in terms of developmental levels and curriculum contexts, let's examine a diversity of examples of organisers that direct learners to differing degrees of depth and breadth within the context of chemicals. The outcomes embedded within the series of organisers presented directly relate to the TAFE course RTC3704A — Prepare and apply chemicals.

RTC3704A prepare and apply chemicals: sample 1

Characteristics / Diversity	physical	behavioural		environmental	S. W. SW		
	what is the chemical?	cause why use this chemical?	effect impact of using this chemical?	where describe the environment which would warrant the use of this chemical?	strengths of the chemical choice	weaknesses of the chemical choice	so what ideas for the use of this chemical
chemical 1							
chemical 2							
chemical 3							
chemical 4							

The above *thinkchart* example explicitly engages the learner in analytical and evaluative thinking as the causes and effects of the chemical are addressed. Additional analysis and evaluation is framed within the organiser as the learner considers the strengths and weaknesses of the specific chemical. Finally, synthesis thinking is achieved as the learner identifies appropriate contexts for the chemical in question.

On the following pages, a number of further example organisers have been provided for your examination. Each one will progressively deepen and broaden the thinking of the learner through the framing of its design. As the sophistication of the thinking increases, so too will the learner's ability to design effective chemical solutions.

27

RTC3704A prepare and apply chemicals: sample 2

Characteristics / Diversity	physical what is the chemical?	behavioural		environmental **where** describe the environment which would warrant the use of this chemical?	S. W. SW		
		cause why use this chemical?	**effect** (+ and -) impact of using this chemical?		strengths of the chemical choice	weaknesses of the chemical choice	*so what* ideas for the use of this chemical
chemical 1		C C C	+ -				
chemical 2		C C C	+ -				
chemical 3		C C C	+ -				
chemical 4		C C C	+ -				

Use of the above *thinkchart* would result in a greater degree of analysis and evaluation. The organiser explicitly directs the learner to consider multiple causes for the use of each specifically named chemical. It also invites the learner to identify possible positive and negative effects of each chemical. While some learners may outline multiple causes and the positive and negative effects on the prior organiser, it is likely that many will not. By explicitly framing the organiser for the inclusion of these aspects, the learner is 'set up' to investigate at a deeper, more comprehensive level.

The following two organisers will increase the thinking of the learning considerably. The sample organiser will comprise three pages, and sample 4 will comprise of four pages. A perforated line within the organiser indicates where the next organiser will attach. It is critical that the sheets be attached to one another as 'organised information facilitates thinking'. When a learner can clearly see all data at a glance, their ability to analyse, evaluate and synthesise is increased.

RTC3704A prepare and apply chemicals: sample 3

characteristics / diversity	physical — what is the chemical?	cause — why use this chemical?	behavioural — immediate	consequences & sequels* — immediate / effects + short term / long term	effects – short term / long term
chemical 1		(((			
chemical 2		(((			
chemical 3		(((			
chemical 4		(((			

RTC3704A prepare and apply chemicals: sample 3 (cont.)

physical				
reactive strategies?				
proactive strategies?				
hazards?				
equipment?				
clean-up?				
application?				

RTC3704A prepare and apply chemicals: sample 3 (cont.)

so what ideas for the use of this chemical			
S. W. SW weaknesses of the chemical choice?			
strengths of the chemical choice			
Environmental describe the environment which would warrant the use of this chemical			

RTC3704A prepare and apply chemicals: sample 4

diversity / characteristics	physical what is the chemical?	cause why use this chemical?	behavioural effects + time	money	environment	consequences & sequels* safety
chemical 1						
chemical 2						
chemical 3						
chemical 4						

RTC3704A prepare and apply chemicals: sample 4 (cont.)

environmental — describe the environment which would warrant the use of this chemical	effects – safety	environment	money	time

RTC3704A prepare and apply chemicals: sample 4 (cont.)

physical				
reactive strategies?				
proactive strategies?				
hazards?				
equipment?				
clean-up?				
application?				

RTC3704A prepare and apply chemicals: sample 4 (cont.)

S. W. SW *so what* ideas for the use of this chemical				
weaknesses of the chemical choice?				
strengths of the chemical choice				

C & S consequences and sequels © Edward de Bono/ *thinkchart* and *S.W.SW* © Lane Clark

As discussed earlier, within the framing of the organiser lies the degree of rigour and sophistication of thinking. Each of the organisers shared within the previous pages were framed differently; consequently the thinking elicited with the use of each one would be significantly different. While it is possible that some students would engage in the thinking framed within the most complex of the organisers presented, it is likely that many would not. By framing an organiser to include exactly what is required in regard to the knowledge and thinking, all learners are 'set up' for greater success! Further organisers will be provided for your use and reference within the final section of this book. At this time, let's move forward on our journey toward developing a deeper understanding of thinking as a process.

While the *thinkchart organiser* explicitly and innately engages the learner in processing (analysis, evaluation and synthesis), it is the cyclical and adaptive nature of the *Clark real thinking process* that is critical if one is to achieve the depth and breadth of knowledge and understanding required for far transfer or high level synthesis. This repetition in thinking can be achieved naturally by using the *Clark thinkit* and *thinkitgreat processes*.

The *Clark thinkit process* is a framework that enables a learner to discover the characteristics of literally anything. The *Clark thinkit process* can be used to discover the characteristics of a fairytale; the characteristics of a graph; the characteristics of classical music; the characteristics of fitness or the characteristics of a chemical management strategy. Simply put, learners can determine what any 'it' is. With the addition of another step, 'great' characteristics can be easily identified. The diagram illustrates the nature of these models on page 36.

the Clark *thinkitgreat* process

1.	Learners investigate their focus, using a diversity of tools for 'finding out' (i.e. field work, CD, internet, video, audio, experts etc.) A conscious attempt should be made to ensure that the finding out experience is multisensory, interactive and diverse. One **thinkchart** is completed and a beginning base of knowledge and understanding is developed. A second investigation is conducted. The processing associated with the use of the *thinkchart* results in the development of further depth and breadth of knowledge and understanding .
2. Hypothesis	A **venn diagram** is used to compare data obtained from the investigation. (Note: Hula Hoops and post it notes can be used as tools to simply and effectively facilitate this aspect of the investigation; paper, pencils; draw software/computer can also be used to assist in the completion of the venn; ideally, learners should be offered a diversity of tools and encouraged to self-select the best tools for their job.) **Data which are shown within the centre of the venn indicates the hypothesis of what 'it' is.** Due to the limited nature of the investigation thus far, further exploration is required before a conclusion can be reached. The analysis, evaluation and synthesis inherent in this aspect of the framework further promotes the development of knowledge and understanding.
3. CHARACTERISTICS 'it'	Further analysis and evaluation occurs through the use of a **cross classification chart.** The hypothesis is tested against further samples to safeguard against a limited investigation. **Those characteristics which are found in ALL samples explored become the learner's foundation for the conclusion and the identification of 'it'.** The learner has found out, analysed, evaluated and synthesised multiple times. Depth and breadth of knowledge and understanding has grown over time through the explicit, cyclical processing which is promoted within the *thinkit* framework.
4.	Learners are provided an opportunity to internalise new learning. This can be done using strategies and tools which are individual to the learner (i.e. quiet reflection; down time; physical activity; diagrams; pictures; drama or re-writing). Learners are invited to share what they now know. Summative evaluation can be administered at this time.
5. 'great' criteria = **it**+☺–☹+💡='it great'	Learners have determined the characteristics of their focus. They have determined what 'it' is. Should they wish to identify GREAT characteristics, one further step is required. Learners are invited to revisit the *thinkchart* organisers used during their initial investigation. Individually, learners are encouraged to add to their 'it' list, both the strengths and ideas outlined within the S and SW aspect of their *thinkchart*; learners may also eliminate any weaknesses identified within the W section of the organiser provided that an 'it' element is NOT omitted. Learners have now outlined 'itgreat'...a personalised list of characteristics which maintain the integrity of what 'it' is while recognising and respecting personal thinking. If the *thinkitgreat* process has been used to determine criteria, teachers are encouraged to format the characteristics into a rubric. This will enable learners to meet the criteria at a level commensurate with their ability; quality, depth, breadth and sophistication can be manipulated within the context of the rubric.

I have included an example of the *Clark thinkitgreat process* in an effort to more clearly illustrate its workings. The content of this example is irrelevant and has been selected purposefully so that the process is not impeded by any complexity. Transfer into more complex contexts will be considered following the completion of the sample *thinkitgreat process*.

model *thinkchart* — investigating fairytales

Characteristics / Diversity	P physical	B behavioural — C cause why? OPV author	B behavioural — E effect impact?! OPV audience	E environmental setting	plot	strength	weakness	so what idea
Beginning Words Once upon a time...	LRHC lived...one day	C begin the story/set the scene	E we know story has begun	HC's house	⊸	I know it's not real	not what I expect	use: once upon a time
Victim hurt	LRHC (person) Poa Poa (person)	C because they are young and old and maybe vulnerable	E we feel bad for them	HC's house Forest Poa Poa's		I liked that HC was young and a girl	the boys might not like it	make a boy and girl victim
Villain baddy	Wolf (animal)	C he has big sharp teeth and is vicious	E we don't like him	Forest Poa Poa's			too many wolves are bad guys	think of a new animal
Hero goody	Herbalist (person)	C he makes potions	E we think he might make a potion for LRHC and PP	Poa Poa's		he's an unusual hero		make my hero be unusual
Problem	Wolf is hungry eats LRHC + Poa Poa	C a resolution is needed	E we are in suspense	Forest Poa Poa's		we're in suspense		
Resolution	Herbalist - medicine to wolf wolf burps up LRHC + Poa Poa	C to make the villain unsuccessful	E we know the victims are OK	Poa Poa's		the wolf loses but isn't killed		make baddy be taught a lesson
Magic	Talking wolf Magic medicine LRHC + PP burped up whole	C so LRHC & PP can be saved	E we know—happy ending	Poa Poa's		funny		have my goody use medicine
Abuse	Wolf tricks LRHC Wolf eats PP Wolf eats LRHC	C to create a problem	E we feel suspense	Forest Poa Poa's		wolf ate them whole	they could come back whole	make sure abuse can be fixed
Ending Words ...happily ever after.	... they lived happily ever after	C to show the villain loses and victim wins	E we're happy	Poa Poa's		we know all is fine	the wolf isn't happy	make baddy happy too - teach lesson
		C	E					
		C	E					

LRHC = Little Red Happy Coat (A Chinese Fairytale)   PP = Poa Poa   OPV © Edward de Bono   laneclark©

deconstruction #1 using the *thinkchart* organiser results in a first layer of depth and breadth in the learner's foundation of knowledge

model *thinkchart* — investigating fairytales: Hansalito and Gretalita (A Spanish Fairytale)

Characteristics / Diversity	P physical	B behavioural (cause why? OPV author / effect impact?! OPV audience)	E environmental setting	plot	strength	weakness	so what idea
Beginning Words Once upon a time...	Once there were	C begin the story/set the scene E we know story has begun	H & G house	(plot)	I know it's not real	not what I expect	use: once upon a time
Victim hurt	Hansalito Gretalita (people)	C because they are young and vulnerable E we feel bad for them	H & G house Forest Susanna's house	(plot)	I liked that there was a boy and girl		make a boy and girl victim
Villain baddy	Stepmother Susanna (people)	C she is a mother and is older she is a witch E we don't like him	H & G house Susanna's house	(plot)		a stepmum shouldn't hurt her kids	don't send a bad message with the villain
Hero goody	Gretalita & Hanselito	C to show kids can be heroes E a victim can take control	H & G house Forest Susanna's house	(plot)	great the victims turn into the heroes		make my victim become a hero
Problem	Stepmother - food sends H + G into woods Susanna is hungry tries to eat Hanselito + Gretalita	C a resolution is needed E we are in suspense	H & G house forest Susanna's house	(plot)	we're in suspense		
Resolution	Gretalita pushes witch in oven	C to make the villain unsuccessful E we know the victims are OK	Susanna's house	(plot)		the victims do wrong as well	don't show that two wrongs make a right
Magic	Candy house Susanna turns into witch	C to make the story interesting E we want to read on	Susanna's house	(plot)	I like a candy house!		
Abuse	Stepmother abandons children Susanna cages them + threatened their lives	C to create a problem E we feel suspense	H & G house Forest Susanna's house	(plot)			
Ending Words ...happily ever after.	Dad finds H & G in forest ...they had a party	C to show the villain loses and victim wins E we're happy	Forest	(plot)	we know all is fine	what happened to the stepmum	answer all the questions at the end
		C E		(plot)			
		C E		(plot)			

OPV © Edward de Bono

laneclark©

deconstruction #2 using the *thinkchart* organiser results in a second layer of depth and breadth

the *thinkitgreat* process — venn diagram: comparing fairytales

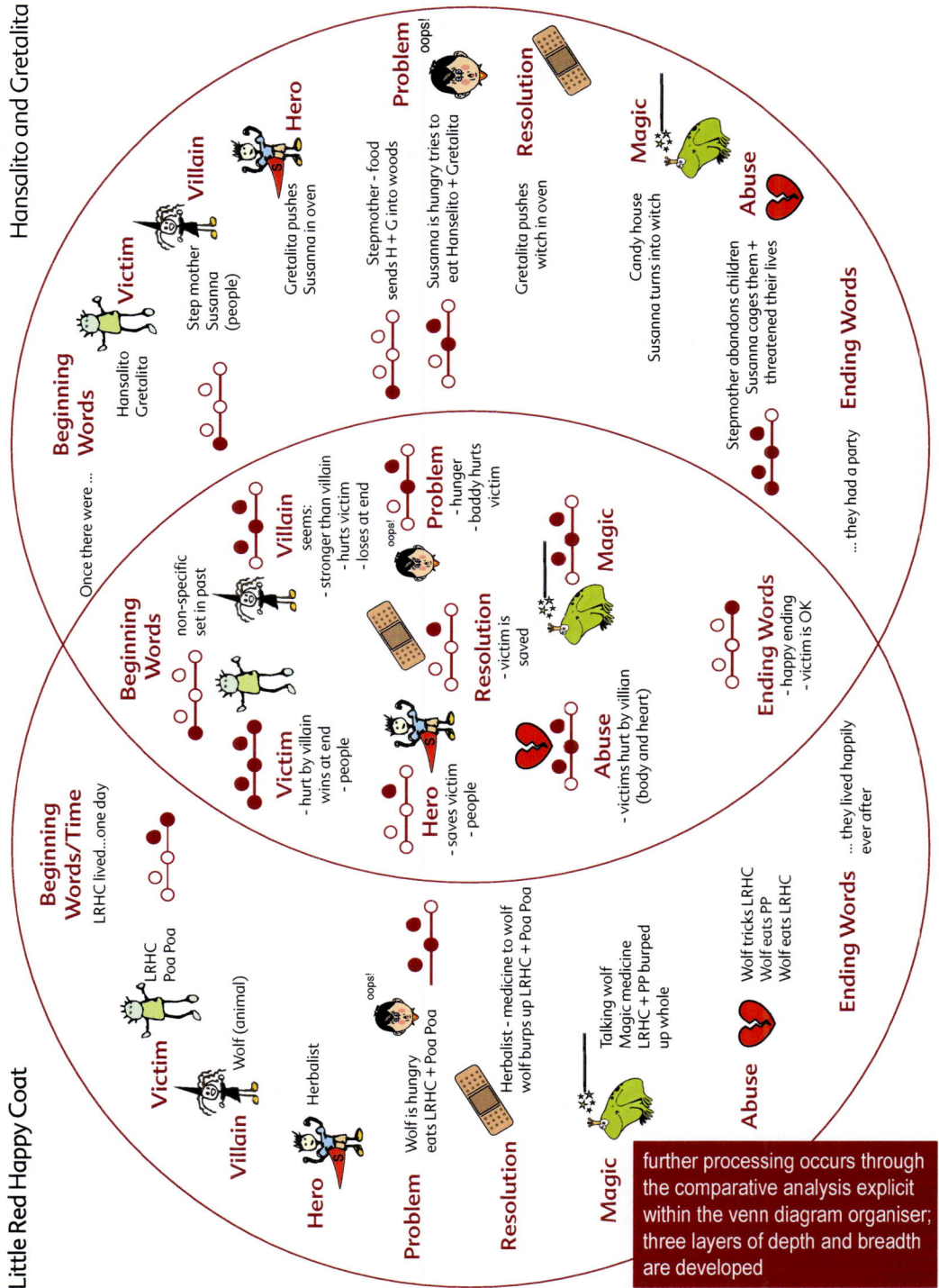

Hansalito and Gretalita

Hero

Villain

Victim
Step mother
Susanna
(people)

Gretalita pushes
Susanna in oven

Problem oops!

Stepmother - food
sends H + G into woods

Susanna is hungry tries to
eat Hanselito + Gretalita

Resolution

Gretalita pushes
witch in oven

Magic

Candy house
Susanna turns into witch

Abuse

**Beginning
Words**
Hansalito
Gretalita

Stepmother abandons children
Susanna cages them +
threatened their lives

... they had a party **Ending Words**

Once there were ...

Villain
seems:
- stronger than villain
- hurts victim
- loses at end

Problem
- hunger
- baddy hurts
victim
oops!

Magic

**Beginning
Words**
non-specific
set in past

Resolution
- victim is
saved

Victim
- hurt by villain
wins at end
- people

Hero
- saves victim
- people

Abuse
- victims hurt by villian
(body and heart)

Ending Words
- happy ending
- victim is OK

... they lived happily
ever after

Little Red Happy Coat

**Beginning
Words/Time**
LRHC lived...one day

Victim
LRHC
Poa Poa

Villain
Wolf (animal)

Hero
Herbalist

Problem
Wolf is hungry
eats LRHC + Poa Poa
oops!

Resolution

Herbalist - medicine to wolf
wolf burps up LRHC + Poa Poa

Magic
Talking wolf
Magic medicine
LRHC + PP burped
up whole

Abuse

Wolf tricks LRHC
Wolf eats PP
Wolf eats LRHC

Ending Words

further processing occurs through
the comparative analysis explicit
within the venn diagram organiser;
three layers of depth and breadth
are developed

the *thinkitgreat* process — cross classification chart: comparing fairytales/testing the hypothesis (guess)

		Beginning Words non-specific past	Victim hurt by villain a person	Villain baddy stronger than victim hurts victim loses at end	Hero saves victim goody	Problem hungry villain	Resolution victim is saved from being eaten	Magic	Abuse victims hurt by villain (body and heart)	Ending Words victim wins villain loses happy ending
								further processing occurs through the analysis and evaluation explicit within the cross checking done with the cross classification chart organiser; the learner has achieved a fourth layer of depth and breadth in their foundation of knowledge		
hypothesis / **diversity**										
fairytale # 3 Cinderella		✓	✓	✓	✓	✗ jealous villain Cinderella can't go to the ball	✗ not really saved but wins	✓	✓	✓
fairytale # 4 3 Pigs		✓	✗ not a person	✓	✓	✓	✓	✓	✓	✓
fairytale # 5										

© 2009 Hawker Brownlow Education HB3522

the *thinkitgreat* process — 'it' list and 'itgreat' list developed by the learner

fairytale 'it' list

☐ **Beginning Words —** Non-specific time
        — Set in past

☐ **Victim —** Gets hurt by villain

☐ **Villain —** baddy hurts victim/loses at end

☐ **Hero —** goody saves victim

☐ **Problem**

☐ **Resolution**

☐ **Magic —** usually with resolution

☐ **Abuse —** usually with problem

☐ **Ending Wording —** happy ending

> the learner determines the base characteristics of a fairytale ... this is their 'it' list

my fairytale 'it GREAT' list

add my
- make my villain get taught a lesson
- make sure my victim can be victimised by the villain

delete my
- don't have any death
- don't have a beautiful victim and an ugly villain
- don't have the words, 'once upon a time' and 'happily ever after'

add my
- make my villain be taught a lesson by the victim
- have my villain come back as the hero in my sequel
- have girl and boy characters to increase readership
- have my victim beautiful on the inside but a little homely on the outside
- think of original opening and closing words

> by adding the strengths, deleting the weaknesses and adding their *so what* ideas from the *S.W.SW* evaluation on their *thinkcharts*, the learner develops their personal 'itgreat' list

model *thinkchart* — investigating fairytales

My Fairytale Criteria

Column 1 (three stars)

- Include beginning words non specific set in past
- Include characters
  - a victim who gets hurt by the villain
  - a villain who hurts the victim and loses at the end
  - a hero who saves the victim
- Justify your characters **WHY?** why did you choose that victim? why that villain? why that hero?
- Include a problem with abuse
- Justify the problem you chose **WHY?**
- Include a resolution with magic
- Include a happy ending

Column 2 (two stars)

- Include beginning words non specific set in past
- Include characters
  - a victim who gets hurt by the villain
  - a villain who hurts the victim and loses at the end
  - a hero who saves the victim
- Justify your characters **WHY?** why did you choose that victim? why that villain? why that hero?
- Include a problem with abuse
- Include a resolution with magic
- Include a happy ending

Column 3 (one star)

- Include beginning words non specific set in past
- Include characters
  - a victim who gets hurt by the villain
  - a villain who hurts the victim and loses at the end
  - a hero who saves the victim
- Include a problem with abuse
- Include a resolution with magic
- Include a happy ending

laneclark©

the teacher develops the base criteria into a rubric and learners negotiate

While the fairytale content in this particular *thinkitgreat process* example is simplistic and perhaps irrelevant in regard to your teaching and learning area of focus, it is the process itself that is important. The *thinkitgreat process* is transferable to any context where the purpose is to examine and extract the characteristics or elements. When students are simply 'told' the elements, new knowledge is rarely internalised and often only superficially retained. When a learner is enabled and empowered to discover new information for themselves and, as importantly, explicitly process this data, personal meaning making is promoted. Deeper knowledge and understanding is obtained; learning is more likely retained; and, most critically, available for application at a level of depth and breadth commensurate with understanding.

The following example is in reference to the TAFE course RTC5702A. Element 2 directs students to develop a chemical risk management strategy. The strategy must be developed in accordance with the legislation and the Integrated Pest Management (IPM), Integrated Resistance Management (IRM) and Integrated Animal Health Management (IAHM) principles. Included within the strategy must be the following:

- hazards associated with the transportation, storage and handling of chemicals
- risk factors associated with the use of chemicals
- risk controls measures in accordance with regulatory requirements

Learners can be 'set up' to meet this competency in one of two ways:

They can learn about each aspect, enter into discussions and then eventually develop their strategy, giving it their best shot in the hopes of doing so at a competent level.

OR

They can be offered a process which enables them to analyse and evaluate a diversity of management strategies so that they can identify the similarities and differences between these; evaluate the strengths and weaknesses of each sample; and ultimately design their own strategy, strategically and purposefully, to meet what they have determined to be the characteristics of a GREAT risk management strategy. By providing students with a 'road map' to meet the competency, students are not simply shown *what to learn*, but more importantly *how to learn*. Students are not told *what to do*, but more importantly they are told *how to do*.

The following pages offer an example of how students can use the *Clark thinkit process* to determine the 'characteristics of a chemical risk management strategy'; and then how they can use the *Clark thinkitgreat process* to identify the characteristics of a 'GREAT chemical risk management strategy'. In essence, the *thinkitgreat process* will empower students to develop specific success criteria prior to beginning the design and development of their own strategy.

thinkitgreat — determining the characteristics of a GREAT risk management strategy

Analysis/Evaluation — Components	Physical — What do you see?	Behavioural — Why has this been included/omitted?	Environmental — Where is the component found within the strategy?	Strengths — Strengths of strategy	Weaknesses — Weaknesses of strategy	So What Ideas for my strategy — what?	justification
Controls changing practices							
Controls wearing PPE							
Format # of pages							
Format # sections							
Format general layout							

deconstruction #1 using the *thinkchart* organiser results in a first layer of depth and breadth in the learner's foundation of knowledge

thinkitgreat — determining the characteristics of a GREAT risk management strategy

Analysis/ Evaluation / Components	Physical — What do you see?	Behavioural — Why has this been included/omitted?	Environmental — Where is the component found within the strategy?	Strengths — Strengths of strategy	Weaknesses — Weaknesses of strategy	So *What* Ideas for my strategy — what?	justification
Hazards — transport							
storage							
handling							
Risks — environment							
produce							
people							
Controls — elimination							
substitution							
Isolation							
Engineering Controls							

thinkitgreat — determining the characteristics of a GREAT risk management strategy

Analysis/ Evaluation Components	Physical What do you see?	Behavioural Why has this been included/omitted?	Environmental Where is the component found within the strategy?	Strengths Strengths of strategy	Weaknesss Weaknesses of strategy	So What Ideas for my strategy what?	justification
Controls: changing practices							
wearing PPE							
Format: # of pages							
# sections							
general layout							

deconstruction #2 using the *thinkchart* organiser results in a second layer of depth and breadth

thinkitgreat — determining the characteristics of a GREAT risk management strategy

Analysis/ Evaluation — Components	Physical — What do you see?	Behavioural — Why has this been included/omitted?	Environmental — Where is the component found within the strategy?	Strengths — Strengths of strategy	Weaknesses — Weaknesses of strategy	So What Ideas for my strategy — what?	justification
Hazards — transport							
storage							
handling							
Risks — environment							
produce							
people							
Controls — elimination							
substitution							
Isolation							
Engineering Controls							

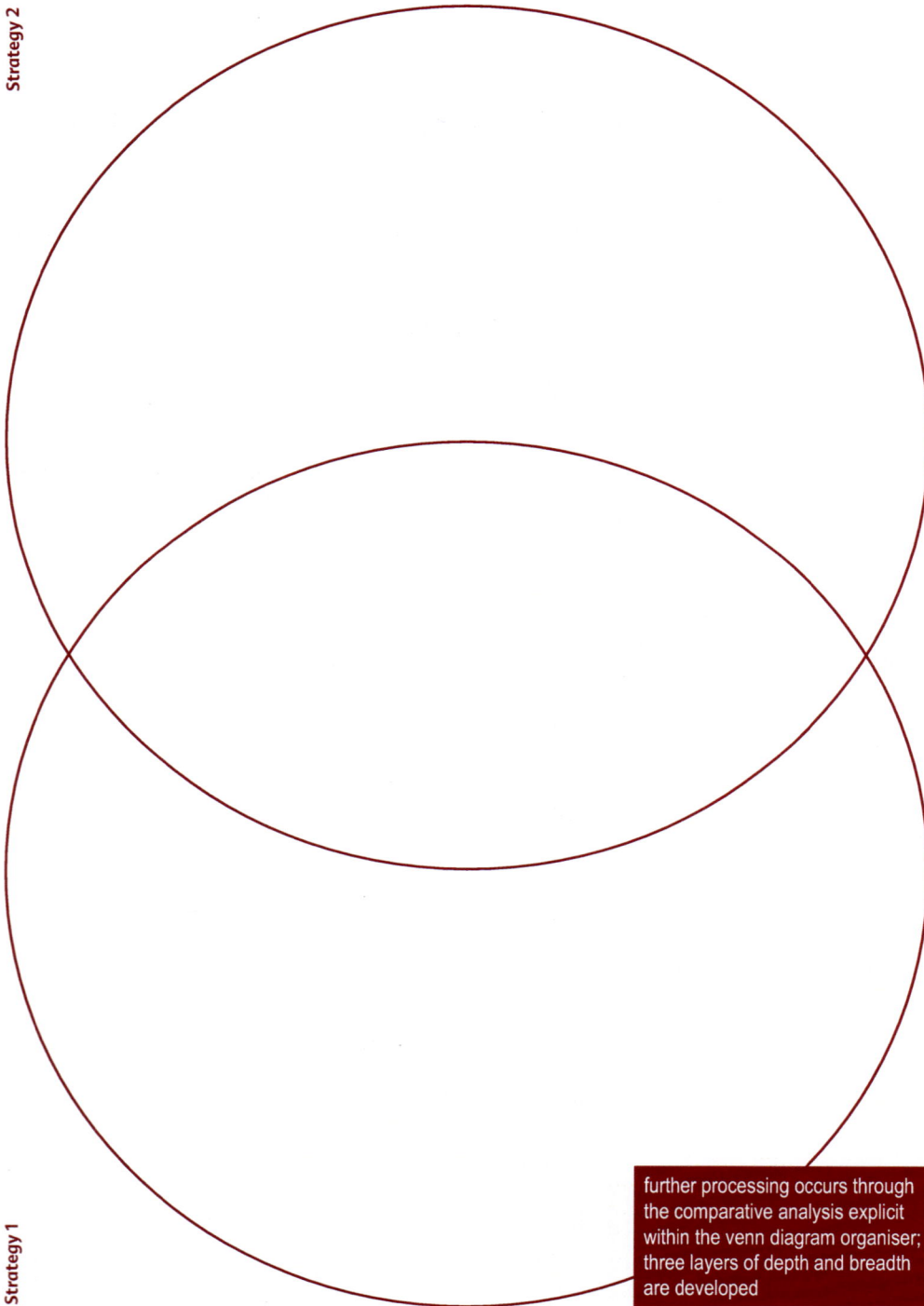

thinkitgreat — analysing risk management strategies: venn diagram

Strategy 2

Strategy 1

further processing occurs through the comparative analysis explicit within the venn diagram organiser; three layers of depth and breadth are developed *thinkitgreat* — evaluating risk management hypothesis: cross classification chart

Hypothesis / Evaluation Against Further Samples											Strengths of sample	Weaknesses of sample	So What Ideas (justify)	
chemical risk strategy 3														
chemical risk strategy 4														
chemical risk strategy 5														

Once students have determined the elements consistent in all Risk Management Strategies, the 'must include' characteristics become clearly evident.

Moreover, the learner's exposure to a diversity of samples, and their personal engagement in 'drawing out' the critical characteristics, results in a level of metacognition and engagement that is not experienced when the teacher simply 'tells' the student these elements. The evaluation of each sample further enhances a student's ability to consciously and strategically design and produce.

This brings us to the actual product that the learner produces. Critical in the production of anything is the justification of the design elements. As per this example, after determining the characteristic of a GREAT Risk Management Strategy, students should be directed to develop their strategy through the use of an explicit publishing framework. The *Clark authorthink publisher's process* is a thinking tool that can be explicitly offered to learners to promote quality publishing. Use of this framework will enhance the student's ability to publish 'quality'. In the planning stage of the framework, learners are expected to develop a plan for the design of their strategy, including justification of each component part. It is in the justification that the learner proves deep or superficial knowledge and comprehension, not in the chemical strategy itself.

The Clark *thinkchart organiser, Clark thinkit* and *thinkitgreat processes* have been introduced as specific thinking tools that can be provided to learners to assist them in comprehensively developing depth of knowledge and depth of understanding. There are, however, literally dozens of thinking tools that can be selected and used to promote thinking. The *Clark thinkbox* and *thinktower* frameworks have been designed to explicitly highlight these tools for our learners. Let's look further into thinking and its relationship to these two thinking models.

an overview of section two, chapter two: about *thinkbox* and *thinktower*

- The *Clark thinkbox* and *thinktower* frameworks have been developed to make thinking explicit for the learner

- *Thinkbox* and *thinktower* identify types of thinking, and the skills, strategies and tools associated with each

- The models make the relationships between thinking tools, strategies and skills explicit to the learner and subsequently empower them to use the models to plan, assess, evaluate, direct and extend their own thinking

- Learners should eventually be empowered to independently use the *thinkbox* or *thinktower* models to plan the thinking tools, strategies and skills needed during their learning inquiries

- The *thinkbox* and *thinktower* frameworks enable teachers (and eventually learners) to design an 'MI' inclusive thinking and learning experience

- The goal of *thinkbox* and *thinktower* thinking and learning is the design and implementation of ideas

chapter two:
about *thinkbox* and *thinktower*

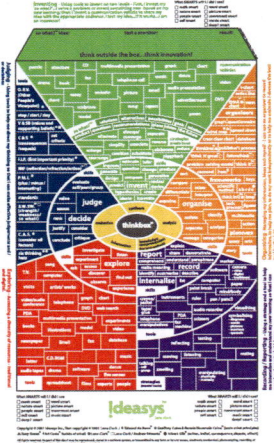

Why? Why do so many of us, as educators, believe that learners can become great thinkers without the explicit teaching of thinking tools, strategies and examples? When we want learners to develop as readers, writers, mathematicians or scientists, we explicitly teach the skills associated with those disciplines; we provide learners with appropriate strategies, tools and, of course, opportunity. When we want learners to develop as thinkers, we invite them to 'go back and think about it' or to 'put on their thinking caps'. We hold unrealistic expectations that learners will develop their ability to think through invitation or opportunity alone. Experience has shown that this is clearly not the case. What if we could provide learners with the tools and strategies associated with different types of thinking?

What if our learners could know and understand the skills, tools and strategies associated with thinking and could evaluate their own thinking, direct their thinking, extend their thinking? This is the purpose and power of the Clark thinkbox and thinktower frameworks.

What? The *Clark thinkbox* and *thinktower* thinking frameworks explicitly identify types of thinking and the skills, tools and strategies associated with each. Both frameworks perform the same function; to assist learners in planning, assessing and evaluating their thinking and learning experiences. By design, the nature of the *thinkbox* best suits thinkers with strong linguistic preferences; while the *thinktower*, although consistent in purpose and method of use to the *thinkbox*, has been designed with visual or pre-reading learners in mind. Teachers demonstrate and use both models in order to meet individual learner preferences.

Developmentally, the frameworks are first used by the teacher to plan, assess and evaluate learning opportunities, then collaboratively by both teacher and learners. Ultimately, learners use the framework independently, as they take control of their learning. Use of these frameworks ensures that thinking skills, tools and frameworks are explicit to the learner throughout the thinking and learning experiences. In turn, greater ownership of the thinking processes will evolve and learners will come to learn how to think for themselves.

deconstructing the *thinkbox* framework

The *Clark thinkbox* model was designed symbolically as a visual reminder of the interconnectedness of thinking. The five types (sections) of thinking intersect at the centre point of the model. Each section contributes to the overall shape of the thinking model and the removal of any aspect of thinking leaves an unbalanced and incomplete model; subsequently representing incomplete thinking.

The framework explicitly depicts the relationship that exists between types of thinking, thinking skills and the tools that can be used to promote both. Use of specific tools results in the proof of the corresponding thinking type and directs the learner to develop the corresponding thinking skills.

As discussed earlier, processing involves a learner's ability to analyse, evaluate and synthesise incoming information. Unfortunately, some teachers limit learners' 'finding out' experiences and simply 'hope' that processing occurs. There is a better way. The *thinkbox* and *thinktower* models can assist teachers and learners to ensure that all learners comprehensively process newly acquired information. The explicit embedding of analysis, evaluation and synthesis tools ensures that all students are strategically 'set up' to engage in the processing required for the development of deep knowledge and understanding. By directing learners to the 'information' section of the framework, and directing them to select a designated number of tools, the chance of a limited or biased 'finding out' experience is minimised. Learners are further enabled by inviting them to self-select their tools and strategies for internalising in the 'knowledge.comprehensive' section of *thinkbox*. Let's take a closer look at each section of the *thinkbox* framework to better understand its power in promoting both thinking and learning.

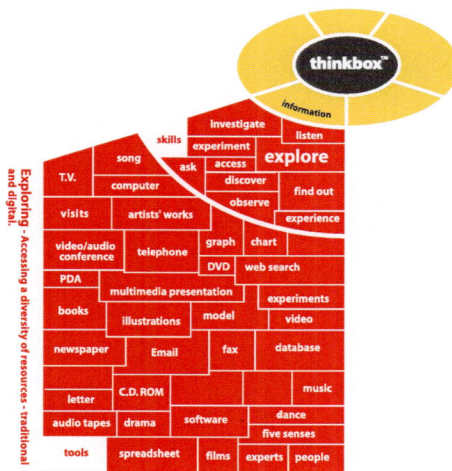

information thinking

The information section at the base of the model explicitly illustrates the importance of the finding out experience. Traditionally, once learners are able to read, they are generally directed to access text based tools. But with all information entering the brain via the five senses, teachers and learners should make experiential experiences and multisensory tools a priority selection when finding out. A diversity of tools for accessing information are identified within *thinkbox* and teachers/learners should be encouraged to select tools which cater to all modalities or intelligences in accordance with Gardner's Theory of Multiple Intelligences (see page 61). By strategically selecting tools and cross checking each selection against the modalities listed below, an inclusive 'finding out' experience is ensured. 'Must use' tools can be identified for learners if specific resources are mandatory. Learners should order their use of tools so that they cater to their strengths before their struggles. This should enable them to use those tools that do not represent their modalities with greater success. Because learners can grow their 'brain map', it is critical that they always use tools which may prove more challenging. Newer and older technologies exist side by side as learners are invited to select the best tool for their learning.

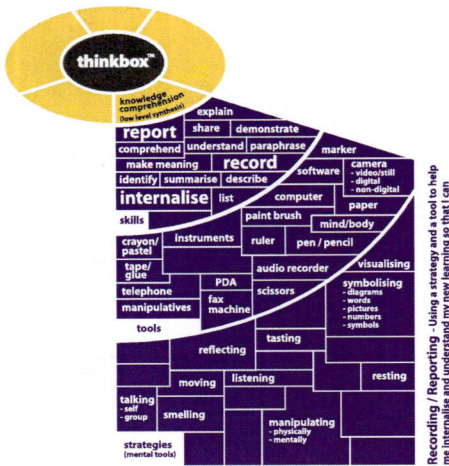

knowledge.comprehension thinking

The knowledge.comprehension section of *thinkbox* offers learners tools and strategies for: recording; internalising; and reporting on newly acquired information.

recording new information

As learners find out, they are directed to record their discoveries using a self-selected strategy and tool. Visual learners may choose to record using symbols, diagrams or pictures; linguistic learners may prefer recording with words. Some learners may choose to use pen and paper; others a computer, audio recorder, video or still camera. The power of *thinkbox* is that it makes explicit a diversity of tools for individual selection. If a 'must do' recording approach is required, learners should be encouraged to use a pre-strategy that works for them beforehand. For example, many learners think more quickly than they write. If writing is the only option available, the learner may write very little or nothing. The provision of an audio recording device as a pre-strategy to writing enables and empowers the learner to speak their thinking. The tape recording can then be started and stopped as required and the written requirement completed in a way that better reflects the abilities of the learner.

internalising new information

The moment the 'finding out' begins, the processing of the new information begins. This is not something we are generally conscious of. Some individuals process well, but many may not. Both *thinkbox and thinktower* can be used to encourage learners to explicitly internalise (process) newly acquired information. During the finding out phase of the learning opportunity, students are directed in their processing through the use of analytical, evaluative and synthesis thinking tools. As detailed in chapter 2, this ongoing processing is crucial in the overall development of deep knowledge and understanding.

To enhance a learner's ability to build upon what they know, and eventually report what they know, it is recommended that they be provided an opportunity to focus exclusively on processing or internalising recently acquired information at regular intervals during the learning process. This exclusive processing time is also provided prior to administering any form of summative assessment. The learner should be encouraged to take time to reflect on their new learning using an internalisation tool and strategy of their choice. Some learners internalise best by engaging in self talk, they require time to reflect internally; others prefer group talk, they need conversation with others in order to make meaning. There are learners who need to re-write notes and others who must re-organise notes into a diagram or flow-chart. Some learners internalise while resting from the learning, going for a run, a bike ride or a walk along the beach. Again, as outlined within Howard Gardner's Theory of Multiple Intelligences, every brain is unique. When individual preferences are catered for, thinking and learning are promoted. All too often, internalisation in school is facilitated through discussion only. If discussion is a course requirement, learners should be encouraged to select a strategy of choice prior to engaging in the must do activity.

reporting new information

After finding out, analysing, evaluating and synthesising what has been discovered, a NEW level of understanding will have been reached. Because 'the parts in a new whole' represent synthesis type thinking, I have 'tagged' this knowledge.comprehension section *low-level synthesis*. A learner's understanding has grown and changed through the processing of new information. However on the synthesis continuum, the learner is far from ready or able to *USE the learning to make a difference in their life or the lives of others*. This degree of 'far transfer' requires a much greater depth and breadth of understanding. Still, from the original level of understanding, a transfer has occurred. I call this low degree of synthesis *near transfer*. Learners can prove this level of transfer by identifying what they now know, summarising it, explaining it or even demonstrating it.

It is a teacher's mandate to check a learner's level of knowledge and understanding. This is achieved by inviting the learner to report what they know. A learner's ability to **identify** knowledge.comprehension proves a nearer transfer than those learners who are able to **demonstrate** new learning; **application** of new learning indicates a farther transfer yet; but the greatest proof of learning will become apparent when far transfer occurs and the learner USES their knowledge.comprehension to solve problems, develop alternatives, recommendations, plans, etc (high-level synthesis). This will become a reality as the process of thinking is repeated cyclically, over time.

When inviting learners to report what they know, individual learner modalities must be considered. If a non-linguistic learner is forced to communicate what they know via a written test, they may not be able to show what they truly know. If a test is a requirement, the learner should be encouraged to use a pre-test strategy prior to completing the must do. If a learner is visual/spatial and completes a mindmap or flow chart before the test, their ability to communicate later via the modality of struggle will be enhanced.

analysis and evaluation thinking

The Analysis and Evaluation types of thinking have been placed in a parallel position to illustrate the simultaneous nature of analytical and evaluative thinking. When one analyses information (looks at the parts), decisions are inherently made. Similarly, when one evaluates, the 'parts' must be considered as judgments/decisions are determined. In my opinion, the two types of thinking are inseparable in all aspects of life (except of course in Bloom's Taxonomy!) As processing occurs, both types of thinking are addressed seamlessly but often loosely or superficially. By providing learners with tools from each of these sections of *thinkbox*, analytical and evaluative thinking become deliberate and more rigorous.

analytical thinking

Tools which direct analytical thinking are explicitly selected from the 'analysis' section of *thinkbox*, and 'built into' each learning opportunity.

organisers

Learners are directed to record newly acquired information on an organiser outlined in the 'analysis' (organise) section of the model. This achieves a number of outcomes: the learner is set up to better analyse information (organised information facilitates thinking); rigour in the investigation is assured through the design and selection of the organiser; and finally, the interconnectedness of thinking is seen and experienced.

As explained in Section 2, Chapter 1, the *thinkchart* tool, through its framing, comprehensively engages the learner in not only the analysis and evaluation of newly acquired learning, but also strategically directs the learner toward synthesis. For this reason, it is recommended that this tool be used consistently to support processing.

The strategic embedding of additional tools in the design of the learning will further enhance processing and set the student up for the development of deeper knowledge and understanding. For example the sample on page 28 illustrates the strategic inclusion of de Bono's consequences and sequels tool.

frameworks

Teachers can provide learners with frameworks in an effort to further promote independent skill application and transfer:

- a publisher's process can be strategically incorporated into the planning of a learning opportunity so that the learner is directed to produce 'quality' when publishing letters, emails, reports, multimedia, etc.
- a problem solving model can be offered to the learner for reference should they meet with challenges during their learning journey
- a sciencing framework can be offered as a support when quality investigation, experimentation, hypotheses or conclusions are required

planners

Planners can also be incorporated into learning opportunities designed for the learner:

- an action plan that itemises tasks, outlines individual student responsibilities within a group and indicates dates/timelines can accompany an inquiry
- a report plan or 'multimedia plan' can be offered, in an effort to promote the address of specific criteria and pre-development thinking

By incorporating these organisers, frameworks and planners into the design of the learning, students 'live' the use of those tools that they are likely to require when learning independently out of the school setting. Further to this, processing is explicitly and deliberately promoted.

evaluative thinking

Again, during processing, evaluative thinking occurs implicitly to varying degrees depending on the learner. However, when teachers incorporate a diversity of tools from the 'evaluation' section of *thinkbox/thinktower* into the design of their learning opportunities, a learner's ability to evaluate and process are heightened because they are using tools that explicitly direct their thinking:

- the inclusion of criteria assists learners in knowing where they are and where they are going; it also promotes responsibility and accountability as learners are directed to self evaluate efforts prior to teacher feedback

- the incorporation of such tools as de Bono's consequences and sequels (C&S) or Clark's strengths, weaknesses and *so what* ideas (*S.W.SW*), into a learning task, empowers students to evaluate information, decisions and/or learning behaviour during their learning journey; this not only sets a learner up to reflect and modify their learning, it promotes evaluative thinking which in turn promotes deep knowledge and understanding

synthesis thinking

Synthesis as a definition suggests that the parts have been developed in a new and different whole. As discussed earlier in Chapter 1 (see p. 9—16), comprehension is actually synthesis, as newly developed understanding represents the original parts in a new whole; application is also synthesis, because when a learner applies new learning, that too is a new and different whole for that learner. While knowledge.comprehension, replication and application represent synthesis type thinking, I want learners to recognise that the transfer from the old to the new is quite near or close. Consequently, I call knowledge. comprehension and application *low-level synthesis*. The synthesis type thinking identified on *thinkbox* is considered *high-level synthesis*, as it represents a far transfer of knowledge. comprehension. Learners have developed depth and breadth of knowledge. comprehension and can subsequently USE their knowledge and understanding to *make a difference in their lives and/or the lives of others*. They can self actualise their new knowledge. Synthesis at this level is evidenced as the pinnacle of thinking. Consequently, high level synthesis type thinking is found at the top of the model.

A purpose for skills, processes and knowledge becomes evident to the learner when high-level synthesis is explicitly incorporated into the planning of a learning experience. Instead of learning for the sole purpose of 'knowing it', teachers plan how learners can take newly acquired information and *use it*. They consider and challenge what learners now know: 'So you know it … *so what*?! How can you USE what you know to make a difference in your life and the lives of others?' With the use of tools such as the *Clark S.W.SW, futurethink* and *thinkitgreat* tools; de Bono's 6 Hats and C&S tools, learners are encouraged to develop solutions to problems they have become aware of; they generate recommendations, alternatives and new possibilities; follow patterns and trends to predict the future; and create new products. It is at this stage of learning that learners invent, change, adapt and design ideas. Learners use a variety of mental tools (i.e. combine, associate, reduce, increase) to assist in their idea generation.

Following the generation of the *so what* idea, learners determine the appropriate audience for their message. Learners consider the most effective communication vehicle for delivery; they develop criteria for that communiqué and begin the design and development process. Rather than finding out *to know* and regurgitate information, learners find out so that they can *use* information! This type of transfer takes time and occurs as a result of the cyclical, adaptive nature of the *Clark real thinking process*. As explained in detail in Chapter 1 (see

p. 9—16) learners MUST be provided with this cycle of repeated opportunities to engage analysis, evaluation and synthesis thinking in order to develop the depth and breadth of knowledge, and understanding, required for high-level synthesis or far transfer.

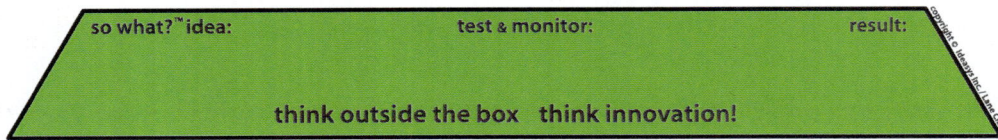

so what?™ idea:	test & monitor:	result:

think outside the box   think innovation!

Innovation

The model further extends synthesis thinking through the very nature of its design. Once learners have used their new knowledge to develop solutions, create products, generate recommendations, etc, they are directed toward **action**. They are cued, within the top portion of the framework, to record their idea, and outline the way in which their idea will be put into action and tested. Results are also documented. The goal of *thinkbox/thinktower* thinking and learning is the creation of ideas that work; ideas that make a difference in the life of the learner and the lives of designated others. Should an idea/invention be unsuccessful, learners are redirected to the analysis and evaluation sections of *thinkbox/thinktower*. Was the lack of success associated with the *so what* idea generated or was the communication vehicle selected inappropriate or ineffective? Goals are set for improvement on their next inquiry effort.

thinktower

The *thinktower* model, although linear in its appearance, has also been designed symbolically as a visual reminder of the interconnectedness of thinking. The five types (sections) of thinking must be incorporated comprehensively into the learning. Failure to do this would result in the 'crashing' of the tower or 'thinking' of the learner.

While the *thinkbox* illustrates thinking in a more authentic manner, littlies have an insatiable desire to 'get to the top'. During prototype trials with both a pictoral *thinkbox* and *thinktower*, young learners consistently gravitated to the *thinktower* model. In order to maintain the structure of their *thinktower*, they learn that they must use tools from each section of their tower. In this way, they live the comprehensiveness of thinking.

thinkbox/thinktower — a tool for reflection, assessment and evaluation

teacher planning

Initially, the *thinkbox* and *thinktower* models are used by the teacher to explicitly plan the thinking tools which will be used by the students during the learning opportunity. Planning with the model ensures that tools are incorporated which represent all types of thinking and all learning modalities. In an effort to enhance processing, tools which promote analysis, evaluation and synthesis are strategically selected for use as the student engages in the finding out experience. Teachers should be mindful to incorporate lower level analytical, evaluative and synthesis tools early in the learning experience as a student's ability to process with depth and breadth develops as their knowledge and understanding develops depth and breadth.

It must be noted that all tools are taught within the context of authentic use. A discrete 'thinking time' is not advocated. As with the learning of any new language, an immersion approach always proves more effective in the long run than a contrived teaching and learning experience. As tools are introduced they are explicitly named, and use of the new thinking vocabulary is encouraged. This practice enhances the learner's ability to accurately and successfully identify the tools used during the tracking experience.

tracking thinking

Following the completion of a learning opportunity that has been planned and implemented by the teacher, students identify the types of thinking, skills, tools and strategies used during the experience by underlining these on their individual black and white *thinkbox* or *thinktower* model. This 'tracking' is modelled by the teacher using a classroom poster size coloured version of *thinkbox* or *thinktower*. (contact office@laneclark.ca for your classroom model of the *thinkbox* or *thinktower* frameworks)

If a specific tool or strategy used does not appear on the thinking model, it can be identified within the blank spaces provided on each model. As learners track on *thinkbox* and *thinktower*, they develop an explicit understanding of the relationships which exist between each type of thinking and its associated skills, tools and strategies. An understanding of the relationship between thinking process and learning process is also promoted as learners reflect on the sequence of tool use. Learners should be encouraged to evaluate the effectiveness of the tools used.

The *S.W.SW* tool can be used by learners to consider the strengths and weaknesses of the tools used. The final SW will direct learners to identify ideas for improving their tool use and/or change their tool use. In doing this, metacognition is promoted.

stages of further use

As learners develop their understanding of *thinkbox/thinktower* and develop their ability to confidently navigate the model, students and teachers use the framework to collaboratively plan learning opportunities. Tracking is consistently undertaken upon the conclusion of the learning in an effort to demonstrate to learners the fluidity of learning. As important as planning is, learning often diverges and requires flexibility! The tools planned and those actually used should reflect a learner's ability to capitalise on learning opportunities that present themselves within the context of the learning process. If the tools planned and those actually used differ too much, this may represent ineffective initial planning. Goals can be identified to improve in this regard. Eventually, learners should be invited to include an 'action plan' to accompany their *thinkbox* or *thinktower* planning. The action plan should outline specific learning tasks, along with timelines and individual learner expectations if students are working within a team structure. By inviting learners to justify their planning decisions, metacognition and more effective planning will be promoted.

with responsibility comes privilege

The ultimate goal of *thinkbox/thinktower* teaching and learning results in learners using the model independently to plan and track their thinking. This is an earned privilege. In order for learners to earn this privilege, they must prove that they understand *thinkbox* and its workings with a degree of depth and breadth. While superficial understanding is demonstrated through simply identifying the tools, strategies and thinking types used during their inquiry (tracking on *thinkbox*), deep knowledge and understanding is proven when they can evaluate the tools and strategies used and can set goals for future tool and strategy selection.

Once learners demonstrate that they do in fact hold this level of knowledge and understanding of the framework, they are invited, individually or in teams, to use their personal *thinkbox/thinktower* model to plan the tools and strategies associated with their learning. A student— teacher conference is conducted prior to the implementation of their plan and modifications made if required; following the completion of the learning opportunity, learners continue to track and evaluate their thinking, and set goals.

Upon reaching this level of independence and self-direction, it is recommended that students be introduced to the *Clark think!nQ real learning framework* as a model which interfaces with the *thinkbox* and *thinktower* thinking frameworks. Use of *think!nQ*, a framework which mirrors the natural stages of the learning process, further promotes thinking and learning skill development, as it adds a dimension of greater sophistication and depth to the learning. A simplified version of this framework will be explored within the next section (see p. 79).

thinkbox and Multiple Intelligences theory

Within the 'information', 'knowledge/comprehension' and 'synthesis' sections of *thinkbox*, a list of Gardner's Multiple Intelligences has been included. Once tools have been identified, teachers (and later students) monitor how 'MI inclusive' their choices have been by referencing these 'MI' lists. This 'cross checking safeguard' enables teachers and learners to plan a holistic learning opportunity. If particular 'intelligences' have been omitted from the tools and strategies planned, adjustments can be made. By addressing as many intelligences as possible in the tool selection process, learners are provided the opportunity to use tools that cater to individual preferences and abilities, whilst also ensuring the use of those tools which they may feel less comfortable with — subsequently stretching the learner.

I would like to take the opportunity at this time to consider more closely Gardner's theory in relation to the *thinkbox* framework.

Gardner's theory was first introduced in 1983. The theory suggests that all human beings have multiple intelligences that can be nurtured, strengthened, ignored and/or weakened. Gardner defines intelligence as: "...the ability to solve problems and fashion products which are valued in one or more cultural groups" .

At this time, Gardner has identified nine intelligences and suggests that there may be more.

Gardner has used the following 8 criteria to identify what constitutes an intelligence:

- a definite area in the brain responsible for the functions of the intelligence has been located
- there are people who demonstrate outstanding ability in the intelligence
- each intelligence has its own special 'way of doing things'
- an intelligence has developmental stages from beginner through to expert
- an intelligence can be seen in other animals or in people who lived many years ago
- each intelligence has tasks which can be done, observed and measured
- an intelligence can be tested by psychometric (mind measuring) tests
- an intelligence has its own symbol system

Lane Clark, 'Kidspeak' translation of 8 criteria, *Frames of Mind* pp. 59—70, 1993.

Copyright 1993; intro to second paper edition (tenth anniversary edition), copyright 1993, published by Basic Books, A subsidiary of Perseus Books LLC

The intelligences are as follows:

LINGUISTIC: aptitude with the spoken and written word and languages

MATHEMATICAL/LOGICAL: aptitude with numbers, problem solving and reasoning

VISUAL/SPATIAL: aptitude to think in pictures and images; visualise abstractly and accurately

BODILY KINESTHETIC: aptitude with 'hands on' experiences, athletics

MUSICAL: aptitude with musical experiences (composition, performance, appreciation)

INTRAPERSONAL: aptitude in understanding oneself (feelings, values, ideas)

INTERPERSONAL: aptitude in understanding and relating to others

NATURALIST: aptitude in understanding and relating to nature

EXISTENTIALIST: aptitude in understanding humankind in the 'big picture' of existence

---

For educators who are interested in the implications of Gardner's theory on classroom practice, special attention must be given to Gardner's definition of 'intelligence'. Many teachers suggest that they are catering to diverse intelligences through the design of classroom opportunities that invite learners to receive and communicate through their preferred modalities. For example, a learner is provided the option of finding out via a book, a video or a model, and may share their understanding of material through a written report, painting or spoken report. While the provision of choice limits fewer learners, this inclusionary approach is simply the beginning of 'MI literate' practice. If learners are not invited to USE their learning to 'solve problems and fashion products', intelligence, as defined by Gardner, is not being promoted and developed.

Teachers must move beyond a classroom program that simply invites the learner to 'find out' and 'report/share/regurgitate'. While these skill sets (accessing information and reporting knowledge and understanding) are critical to a learner's eventual ability to engage in the deep processing required for far transfer, they should provide the springboard for the academic program not the sum total of the learning experience. Once learners have proven what they know, we must encourage them to 'use that knowledge, to make a difference in their life or the lives of others'. This is in fact the real key to enabling Gardner's theory to penetrate the classroom door!

When using *thinkbox/thinktower* to plan learning opportunities, learners are offered a diversity of tools to utilise when accessing information, internalising new learning, reporting understanding, analysing and evaluating learning. The self-selection of tools ensures that learners are catered for in terms of MI preferences while teacher-directed must dos ensure the development of a learner's specific areas of need. When teachers use the thinking frameworks in tandem with the *Clark think!nQ real learning framework* (see the next chapter), learners are invited to USE new learning to solve problems and/or fashion products during the *so what* aspect of each model. The communication of the *so what* to the appropriate audience necessitates the learner, once again, self-selecting tools which best suit not only their MI preference but, as importantly, their audience.

assessment and evaluation of the learner

Let's take a closer look at MI, assessment and evaluation, and one more reason to include *thinkbox* and *thinktower* as an integral part of your teaching and learning program.

Teachers assess and evaluate learners in a diversity of ways, but each involves the learner's ability to share concepts, knowledge and skills in an effort to demonstrate understanding. Having recognised this, a learner can only express or share that which has been received and in fact internalised, making the evaluative process much more complex and holistic than initially outlined. There's more ...

What if a learner is invited to receive, internalise and/or express through a modality that is not theirs? How would this affect the assessment and evaluation of the learner?

CHALLENGE

A teacher is evaluating a learner who struggles linguistically and mathematically but shows aptitude when engaged in 'hands on' pursuits. In which of the scenarios provided would a teacher know that their evaluation is accurate and fair?

1) The learner receives through a linguistic means (i.e. book, spoken info)
   The learner expresses through a bodily/kinesthetic means (i.e. model)
   Is the assessment & evaluation accurate?

   R ⟶ E ⟶ A&E ?

2) The learner receives through a bodily/kinesthetic means (model, 5 senses experience)
   The learner expresses through a linguistic means (i.e. written test, report)
   Is the assessment & evaluation accurate?

   R ⟶ E ⟶ A&E ?

3) The learner receives through a linguistic means (model, 5 senses experience)
   The learner expresses through a linguistic means (i.e. written test, report)
   Is the assessment & evaluation accurate?

   R ⟶ E ⟶ A&E ?

4) The learner receives through a bodily/kinesthetic means (models, 5 senses experience)
   The learner expresses through a bodily/kinesthetic means (i.e. models, drama)
   Is the assessment & evaluation accurate?

   R ⟶ E ⟶ A&E ?

R = Receives   E = Expresses   A&E = Assessment and Evaluation   linguistic learner   bodily/kinesthetic learner

---

R ⟶ E ⟶ A✗E ?

Scenario 1 often leaves teacher and learner 'none the wiser'. Because they are expressing their understanding and knowledge via a modality of strength, both may expect that the evaluation is accurate. However, learners can only express what has been received and in this situation the learner received new information through resources which present difficulty. The end result is inaccurate and invalid assessment and evaluation.

R ⟶ E ⟶ A✗E ?

The learner in Scenario 2 may know and understand the learning but may be unable to demonstrate this due to their limitations in communicating linguistically. This scenario frustrates both learner and teacher as both know they know more - the learner couldn't get it out! The end result is inaccurate and invalid assessment and evaluation.

R ⟶ E ⟶ A✗E ?

Scenario 3 is perhaps one of the most tragic of examples. This learner is both receiving and expressing through modalities of weakness. What chance for success have we really offered this learner? How many of our students have been diagnosed 'at risk', 'learning disabled', 'struggling'? What are the implications for the learner who has been misdiagnosed, labelled unnecessarily and inaccurately? Knowing the effects of stress on academic performance and learning potential, how many learners have been further limited through the very nature of this diagnostic process? The end result is inaccurate and invalid assessment and evaluation.

R ⟶ E ⟶ A✓E ?

The learner who has been provided the opportunity to receive and express in ways which draw on their strengths and abilities is the learner who has been assessed and evaluated accurately, fairly and with validity. The teacher who offers this scenario to the learner is the teacher who 'walks the talk' of MI theory. It is this teacher who empowers the learner to develop 'intelligence' as the solid understanding of new learning is used to 'solve problems and fashion products'.

So how does the teacher do it? How does the teacher possibly cater for each individual learner, ensuring that they receive, internalise and express through modalities that are personal? As promised, let's look to *thinkbox/thinktower* and see how individualisation becomes reality.

mi check

Inventing - Using tools to invent on two levels - First, I invent my 'so what?'...I solve a problem or invent something new based on my new learning; then I invent a communication vehicle to share my idea with the appropriate audience. I test my idea...if it works...I am an innovator!

What SMARTS will I / did I use?
- math smart
- nature smart
- people smart
- self smart
- word smart
- picture smart
- movement smart
- music smart
- deep? smart

so what?™ Idea: test & monitor: result:

think outside the box...think innovation!

Learners take what they have learned to fashion products and solve problems

Judging - Using tools to help me direct my thinking so that I can make effective judgements and / or decisions

Organising - Managing my information, ideas and myself - I can use an organiser to record information, to help me plan, to do my work independently or to help me evaluate. I choose the best tool for the job!

Exploring - Accessing a diversity of resources - traditional and digital.

Recording / Reporting - Using a strategy and a tool to help me internalise and understand my new learning so that I can record and report what I know.

thinkbox™

Ideasys™
lane clark

mi check   **mi check**

What SMARTS will I / did I use?
- math smart
- nature smart
- people smart
- self smart
- deep? smart
- word smart
- picture smart
- movement smart
- music smart

What SMARTS will I / did I use?
- math smart
- nature smart
- people smart
- self smart
- word smart
- picture smart
- movement smart
- music smart
- deep? smart

using *thinkbox/thinktower* to ensure individualisation becomes reality

It is important to note that it is NOT necessary to know the specific modalities of each of your learners. Instead, a well-designed and implemented inclusive program will cater to the needs of all. As teachers, it is critical that our learners are offered a diversity of tools for accessing information; a diversity of tools and opportunities to process that which has been received; and finally, a diversity of tools for communicating what is known.

In learning situations with 'younger' learners, it is often the teacher who organises the tools for accessing, internalising and communicating learning. As learners develop, this responsibility can be taken on by the learner themselves should they feel it would be advantageous. Knowledge becomes power when an individual chooses to USE new knowledge to make a difference.

Use of *thinkbox* and *thinktower* frameworks teach learners how to think AND also enable teachers to effortlessly infuse the Theory of Multiple Intelligences into classroom practice.

When using *thinkbox* or *thinktower* to plan learning opportunities, a diversity of tools are offered to learners to utilise when accessing information, internalising new learning, reporting understanding, and analysing and evaluating learning. This self-selection of tools ensures that learner modalities are catered to, while teacher-directed 'must do's' ensure the development of a learner's specific areas of need. When teachers use the *thinkbox or thinktower* thinking frameworks in tandem with the *Clark think!nQ real learning framework,* learners are invited to USE their new learning to solve problems and/or fashion products during the *so what* aspect of the model. The communication of the *so what* to the appropriate audience requires the learner to self-select tools which best suit their Multiple Intelligence preference while also considering their audience's needs.

Action

1. Reflect on the questions provided on page 62—63. Record your thinking in response to each question. File your responses and date the record. Revisit this task once or twice a year. You will find that as your thinking changes, so too will your practice.

2. Deconstruct the thinking process. How does thinking occur?

3. Outline how you are currently addressing thinking within your classroom. How does it compare to the way you believe thinking occurs?

Extended Challenge

1. Read the scenarios presented on pages 67 and 68. These represent some of the more common ways that teachers are infusing thinking into their classroom practice. Copy and enlarge the pages onto A3; then use the *S.W.SW* organisers provided to consider the strengths and weaknesses of each approach. Capitalise on the strengths you have identified and counter the weaknesses in an effort to design an approach that will work for you.

2. Use the *S.W.SW* tool to outline the strengths and weaknesses of your current approach to thinking. How could you change your approach to further promote deep thinking and understanding? Record your ideas in the SW section of your organiser.

3. Complete a de Bono OPV (other people's viewpoint) in an effort to challenge and/or extend your own thinking. Share the scenarios with a friend and invite your colleague to evaluate each example. I have also evaluated each of the scenarios and have included my organiser for your reference. Read the thinking of others, then revisit your initial thinking. Modify your organiser in accordance with your new thinking.

analysing and evaluating the infusion of thinking — cross classification chart

Thinking / Samples	**S** strengths ☺	**W** weaknesses ☹	**SW** *so what* ideas
example no. 1 • the teacher consciously plans for the use of one to five tools each week			
example no. 2 • a 'thinking time' is timetabled into the week; students are taught thinking tools during this time			
example no. 3 • thinking tools are organised on a developmental continuum; specific tools are introduced at each level or in each year			

analysing and evaluating the infusion of thinking — cross classification chart (cont.)

Thinking / Samples	S strengths 😊	W weaknesses ☹	SW so what ideas 💡
example no. 4 • a limited number of tools are introduced to all students; these are the only tools used but they are regularly used; and are utilised in a diversity of ways			
example no. 5 • the teacher uses the *thinkbox* or *thinktower* thinking frameworks along with the *think!nQ learning process* to design and deliver curriculum			
example no. 6 • record your current approach to the infusion of thinking in your classroom			
example no. 7 • identify an approach not yet noted			

analysing and evaluating the infusion of thinking example — cross classification chart

Thinking / Samples	S strengths ☺	W weaknesses ☹	SW so what ideas 💡
example no. 1 • the teacher consciously plans for the use of one to five tools each week	• teacher is taking responsibility for introducing learners to thinking tools • learners are developing a repertoire of tools over time • teacher is not overwhelmed • learner is not overwhelmed • learner and teacher are developing a shared language	• as teacher introduces 'thinking tools' learners may think they are only thinking when using a tool • learners may not use thinking tool unless designed into learning by teacher	• explain to students that they are thinking all the time but the use of a thinking tool might promote more effective thinking as it explictly directs thinking • explain that you will begin to introduce thinking tools slowly over time and name them so that one day they can self-select their own as required • in an effort to promote transfer, once a tool has been introduced in a formalised context, use the tool on demand whenever it could enhance and support thinking • ensure that the tool you introduce legitimately assists the learner in their thinking; the tool should enable the learner to do their learning task more effectively —relevance will lead to valuing —valuing is necessary for transfer
example no. 2 • a 'thinking time' is timetabled into the week; students are taught thinking tools during this time	• teacher is taking responsibility for introducing learners to thinking tools • learners are developing a repertoire of tools over time • teacher is not overwhelmed • learner is not overwhelmed • learner and teacher are developing a shared language • learners see that the teaching of thinking is valued • learners and teachers are provided an opportunity to focus on thinking; they are not caught up in trying to learn new content or skills as well as a thinking tool • time is provided to think and talk about thinking	• as teacher introduces a 'thinking time' learners may think they are only thinking during their thinking time • learners and teachers may not use thinking tools outside of the designated time	• explain to students that we are taking time each week to focus on thinking; to think about thinking; to develop our thinking skills through the use of thinking tools • use real contexts to introduce the tool to learners • provide learners with a 'thinking journal' and invite them to identify a time throughout the week when the new tool could be used to assist them in their thinking; challenge your students to apply the tool and record in their journal how it went. What worked? What didn't work? What would you do differently next time? What questions do you have? • begin each thinking time with reflection; invite learners to share their transfer experiences; discuss the strengths and weaknesses of the tool introduced the prior week; question and challenge the validity of the tool; identify contexts where the tool might be helpful • create an issues board; ask learners to record on the board learning or thinking challenges that have occurred throughout the week; use the students' issues as the context for future tool introduction and use

analysing and evaluating the infusion of thinking example — cross classification chart (cont.)

Thinking Samples	S strengths	W weaknesses	SW so what ideas
example no. 3 • thinking tools are organised on a developmental continuum; specific tools are introduced at each level	• all teachers must introduce tools; given their choice some may choose not to introduce thinking tools to their learners; this is not an option within this approach • parents, teachers and learners are sent the message that this matters as everyone in the school is participating • learners are provided time to consolidate tools each year before building on repertoire	• this presupposes that thinking tools are developmental and they are not; all learners can use all tools; what needs to be considered is the degree of depth, sophistication and independence involved in the tool use • if the best tool for the job is the Six Thinking Hats®, I actually can't wait until next year to introduce the tool • the year six teacher will have 5 years of tools to learn; some teachers may find it unfair distribution of responsibility (the year one teacher needs to know 4 tools but the year 6 teacher must know 24)	• deconstruct thinking tools for their purpose and the thinking elicited when the tool is used • some tools are more sophisticated than others so once you have done the above, your continuum will be more accurate • explain that each teacher must introduce the tools as outlined on the continuum at their year level but they are NOT restricted to those tools; in this way, teachers who are ready to embed tools more comprehensively may do so

See below for an example of Tool Deconstruction. For more information on tools and their specific relationships to thinking and learning see *Where Thinking and Learning Meet: Tools to Promote Thinking and Learning*, Clark, 2009

Tool Deconstruction Example

tool	thinking	purpose
Plus Minus Interesting (de Bono©)	analysis evaluation emotive	ellicit opinion engage emotionally ellicit questions
Strengths Weaknesses *So What* Ideas (Clark©)	analysis evaluation directed synthesis emotive	ellicit opinion engage emotionally ellicit questions ellicit ideas ellicit relevance
White Hat	knowledge/comp synthesis	ellicit facts ellicit questions
Red Hat	analysis evaluation emotive	ellicit opinion engage emotionally
Yellow Hat Black Hat	analysis evaluation knowledge/comp cognitive	generate an argument based on fact
Green Hat	undirected synthesis	ellicit ideas
Blue Hat (de Bono©)	knowledge/comp analysis evaluation	summarise check for bias check for limited thinking make a decision

Generally, when a learner uses the *S.W.SW* tool or the PMI tool they respond emotionally as they offer an opinion. The Red Hat will achieve this same end. But when using the Yellow and Black Hats, the learner is also directed toward the development of an argument based on fact, not opinion. They are moved from an emotive to a cognitive response.

While the *S.W.SW* tool and PMI tools seem similar, they actually serve different purposes. "This is the plus, this is minus and this is interesting..." Where does that tool lead? The interesting thing is the hmmmmm and this can lead to questions. I will often use this tool during the immersion phase of learning when I am wanting my learners to question. I layer it with a direction to record wonderings in their learning journals.

The final SW of the *S.W.SW* tool leads learners to develop *so what* ideas. This links to their *thinkbox* tool and glossary of *so what* options: alternatives, recommendations, possibilities, a plan, a product, solutions, a vision, a mission. When I am wanting learners to see how they might USE new learning to make a difference in their life or the lives of others, this is my tool of choice. It links the learner to the learning explicitly.

analysing and evaluating the infusion of thinking example — cross classification chart (cont.)

Thinking Samples	S strengths 🙂	W weaknesses 🙁	SW *so what* ideas 💡
example no. 4 • a limited number of tools are introduced to all students; these are the only tools used but they are regularly used; and are utilised in a diversity of ways	• teacher is taking responsibility for introducing learners to limited number of thinking tools • learners are developing competence and confidence with limited tools • teacher is not overwhelmed • learner is not overwhelmed	• learners may not have best tools for the job • learners may not meet potential possible with the use of further tools • learners may get bored and become negative *Note: a hammer is a great tool and very useful; I wouldn't want to build an entire house with a hammer alone*	• we limit our learners by our ignorance; the fewer tools in my repertoire, the fewer tools in theirs • grow your repertoire over time • it is fine to begin slowly but we should have a plan for growth • there are hundreds of thinking tools available for use; reference the bibliography for a number of resources that will assist you in developing your repertoire of tools
example no. 5 • the teacher uses the *thinkbox* or *thinktower* thinking frameworks along with the *think!nQ* learning process to design and deliver curriculum	• teacher is taking responsibility for introducing learners to thinking tools • learners are developing a repertoire of tools over time • learners and teacher are developing a shared language • learners are learning how to think • learners are learning how to learn • learners are living the relationship between thinking and learning • deep knowledge and understanding develop as thinking tools are used in the context of the thinking process • thinking about their thinking and thinking about their learning are embedded within the *think!nQ* process and *thinkbox* tracking • learners learn the language, tools and processes in context through an immersion approach • immersion results in quicker learning and a greater level of transfer	• an immersion approach is more difficult than a compartmentalised approach • teacher may be overwhelmed with the comprehensiveness of the approach	• follow the developmental continuum provided at the back of the book for a step by step guide to changing your thinking and learning approach in a non-threatening way • find a buddy to trial the new approach with • let your learners know that you are learning alongside them • engage in the evaluation of the new approach, tools and processes with your learners as it is through reflection that improvements will occur

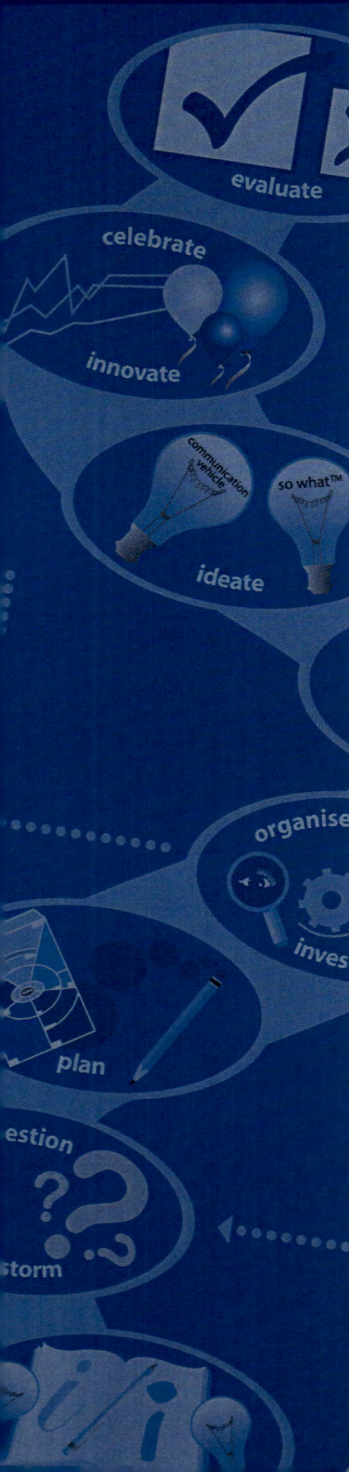

section three

A focus on learning will follow. I will deconstruct the learning process and introduce the *think!nQ real learning framework* as a model that mirrors real life learning.

an overview of section three, chapter one: thinking about learning

- Teaching our learners how to learn must become as important as the knowledge, skills and processes we introduce

- Real learning is initiated by a real purpose

- The purpose is determined at the beginning of the learning process as it drives the learner's need for knowledge, skills and processes

- Real learning goes beyond simply telling others what has been researched and discovered

- Real learning ends in action – the learner can USE his learning to make a difference in his life and/or the lives of others

- The *think!nQ* real learning process was developed after reverse engineering how learning occurs in the real world

chapter one:
thinking about learning

> ... the 'heart of the matter' of any instructional reform or restructuring is the relationship between the teaching and learning processes. We know that effective teaching mirrors effective learning, yet as educators we have not mounted a serious effort to organize teaching around the learning process. Instead, we have viewed education as an institution or an administrative system or a set of instructional techniques (Banathy 1980). We have not examined the learning process and then built instructional systems, administrative systems, indeed entire systems that support what we know about the learning process. We have not built education from the bottom up, so to speak.
>
> —Robert J Marzano,
> A Different Kind of Classroom: *Teaching With Dimensions of Learning*, 2005

It was 1992. I began to question everything I planned and everything I did with my students. The more I questioned, the more uncomfortable I became.

When was the last time, as an adult learner, that I did an animal project?

When was the last time, as an adult learner, that I did an Olympic project? For crying out softly, how many Olympic projects do these kids have to do in the course of their schooling? Throw in the Commonwealth Games, the world cup for this and that. How many flags can a kid make?

When was the last time, as an adult learner, I graphed coloured eyes? Graphed the coloured cars in the parking lot? Graphed heights ... stand up, you're taller than me ... why do I need to graph that?

The more I challenged, the more discomfort I felt.

My students were doing 'projects'. Many times they picked their focus areas. After all, I was 'child centred'. After weeks of research, the unit would end when the kids shared their findings through a self-selected communication vehicle. Again, I was 'child centred' and mindful of learning styles, so some students might share via a picture poster, others through PowerPoint presentations, and perhaps through a diorama. On the surface this sounded fine but with thoughtful reflection I questioned who would hire a person who could only tell them what they already knew, even if it was communicated through multimedia? When my students shared their findings creatively, they did so to their peers as the audience. Does this make sense? After weeks of participating in the same research, they all 'regurgitate' to one another what they discovered. Of course they were disengaged and bored silly! Why did I do this? I wanted to provide them with an opportunity to formally communicate, but was there another way to achieve this aim? How could I offer my learners the opportunity to communicate with real purpose to an authentic audience?

I knew that I wanted to change. I knew that I needed to change — but how? Recognising the whole to be greater than the sum of its parts I queried how I might offer the whole to my learners. I decided to consider how learning occurred in the 'real world'. I needed to get outside of the contrived, unauthentic world of my current classroom, school experience and reality. If I could reverse engineer how I learned outside of school, perhaps I could find a way forward. My deconstruction of the learning process began ...

Thinking About Learning...

- What does it mean to learn?
- Is there a difference between knowing and learning?
- What is authentic learning?
- Where does learning begin?
- What are the natural stages of learning?
- How does one navigate indepth through these stages?
- What tools assist the journey?
- Where does it end?
- How does it end?
- Does it end?

Deconstructing the learning process

While this journey of deconstruction began in 1992, it is a journey that I find myself on to this day. With years of reflection behind me, I can now articulate, with greater precision, my thinking about learning and the changes that have occurred in my practice as a result. I suppose it is worth mentioning that the changes were subtle at first. As my thinking continued to change, so too did my practice. The approach I am sharing with you on these pages is the representation of where I am at today. It is my sincere hope and expectation that my thinking will continue to change. I anticipate the ways in which my approach will mirror these changes over time and look forward to sharing that journey with you in what will become subsequent editions of this book.

Where does learning begin? With a desire, a need, an interest? No. You don't know what you don't know and so how could I want, or desire what I have never heard of? I realised at this point that learning actually began with immersion. We are 'muddied in muck'; we hear something, see something, read something. Immersion leads to awareness, awareness to reflection, and reflection to questioning ... Do I need this? Do I want this? Am I interested in this? If there is no purpose, no interest, no need for the learning, it is likely not pursued. To help me better illustrate this reverse engineering, I would like to share a story that assisted me in crystallising my thinking about learning.

Many years ago, a good friend returned from an overseas trip to New Zealand, Australia and part of Asia. She visited to share her photographs. I was interested in her photos. I made all the right sounds, "Ooooh ... ahhh". When I finished viewing her pictures I gave her a kiss, let her know how pleased I was that she was home safe and made plans to see her the following day. I was interested in her photos. But were they relevant?

I believe, as teachers, that we confuse interest and relevance. I also believe very strongly that if all a learner has as they move into new learning is interest, when the going gets tough the interest will wane.

Let me continue ...

Years later I was invited to Australia for the first time and I thought of my friend. I called her to see if she could come for a visit and bring along her photos.

"What photos?" she asked.

"The ones from Australia," I replied indignantly.

"I don't know where those are."

"Find them ... the wine's chilling!"

All of a sudden her photographs were relevant. I looked at them again for the first time. I saw an image of my friend scuba diving. I asked her when she learned to dive and she happily explained her desire to see the Great Barrier Reef. She explained how this would be the chance of a lifetime and that few areas in the world could match the beauty. I began to see a new possibility for myself while in Australia.

The questions flowed without question starters and prompts for fat vs skinny questions. It is amazing the questions that surface naturally when a learner sees relevance. Many of my initial questions were superficial but completely necessary, I might add. I realised that it was answers to these superficial questions that laid the foundation for the richer questions to follow. Where is the Reef? How did you get there? How long did the course take? Where did you take the course? What did the course cost? Where did you stay? How much were your flights? As she answered my early questions, I realised that there was much to investigate if I was to successfully prepare myself to dive the Reef. You see all major inquiries are laden with petite inquiries. Prioritising is a natural and necessary skill set. Of course one could use a de Bono F.I.P (first important priority) tool at this time to assist them in their thinking task. Before I worried about how to get myself to the Great Barrier Reef, I needed to sort out timeframes. When would I be finished my work in Australia and when was I required to be back in Canada? I needed to find out how I could take the course while on the road. Where would I do my pool dives? Where would I complete my course work? My questions were not arbitrary, they were strategic. Each question led to an investigation that would eventually enable me to achieve the purpose of the learning journey I would experience.

purposeful learning

This brings me to purposeful learning. I identified the purpose of the learning BEFORE I began the journey. I did not do research for the sake of research so that I could share it with my peers. I did not do the research just in case I wanted to use my knowledge years down the road. I did not do my research to ask *why*, once I had completed that research. I researched as a means to an end, and I repeat, I knew the end BEFORE I began the journey. My purpose would drive the investigations, the skills I needed to obtain, the content knowledge I needed to master, the processes I needed to engage in.

I determined my purpose, I asked the strategic questions required to meet my 'endcome'. I organised my investigations and prioritised them. My friend did not put lesson plans together for me. She did not create learning activities for me. She did, however, guide me, make suggestions, question me and redirect me at times. For the first time, 'facilitator' began to make real sense to me.

Could I do this with my students?

Eventually I completed my necessary investigations. I had booked my tests and I was ready to take them. Interestingly, if I had felt unsure of my readiness level for the test I would have cancelled it and rebooked. This is what adults do in the real world. Outside assessment is often a fact of life. However, we generally self assess prior to an outside assessment and make date changes as required.

Could I do this with my students?

Ok, I took my tests. First a written test; then the practical test in the pool. I passed! So what did I do then? I made a puppet play about everything I had learned and shared it with my partner ... I made a picture poster illustrating what I had learned and I shared it with my dad. Of course this is ridiculous but unfortunately, it is what occurs in too many of our classrooms internationally. Kids find out so that they can share their learning in 'powerpointless' presentations and 'diarrhea dioramas'. In real life, once I had found out all that I needed and had passed my required tests, I used my new learning to make a difference in my life. My learning ended in action!

Could I do this with my learners?

It was at this time that I also recognised the difference between ideation and innovation. You see, I had an idea. I wanted to dive the Reef; I wanted to give myself a new experience; I wanted to make a difference in my life. If I entered the water only to find myself nervous to the point where I had to come to the surface before seeing anything I would not have made the intended difference in my life. I realised that ideas were great but, ultimately, ideas required implementation, monitoring and evaluation. Was the intended result achieved? The innovation is the idea that works!

Could I do this with my learners?

I communicated my learning informally with my father. I rang him in Canada and talked a mile a minute, sharing what I had seen and how the experience felt. I did not 'find out' how to dive so that I could share it with my dad. I communicated as a byproduct of my experience. My sharing was completely informal and unrehearsed. I did not focus carefully on my diction, pronunciation, vocabulary use, pacing and intonation. Suddenly I realised that all too often my learners were expected to formally communicate the conclusion of their investigations. Perhaps this was not necessary. Perhaps, discerningly, learners should decide when to communicate formally and when to do so informally.

Could I do this with my learners?

How did the learning all end? I evaluated the diving experience in terms of the difference it did or did not make in my life but I also considered so much more in my reflections. What went well? What was less than acceptable? Would I go back to that area of the Reef? Would I use that accommodation again? Did I enjoy the experience enough to do it again? At times, the learning might seem 'over', for a period of time anyway. At times this evaluation might lead to the identification of new possibilities for further learning. Am I interested in taking part 2 of my qualification? What is involved in achieving this? The cycle of learning is new again.

Could I do this with my learners?

Could I change the way I design and deliver curriculum so that the learning process becomes as important as learning knowledge, understandings, processes and skills? Could I provide my learners with a concrete model of the process so that they become cognisant of the stages? Could I enable and empower my learners to one day use this process, independently and self-directedly, to learn literally anything they desire?

Chapter 2 will introduce to you the model that was created as a result of this reverse engineering or deconstruction. I call it the *Clark think!nQ* (think inquiry) *real learning process.*

an overview of section three, chapter two: about *think!nQ*

- The *Clark think!nQ real learning framework* identifies the stages of the natural learning process

- Use of the *think!nQ* framework teaches learners how to learn, independently, through a process that mirrors real life thinking and learning

- The *think!nQ* framework empowers teachers to integrate authentically and move beyond the delivery of 'themes'

- By teaching our kids how to learn we can seamlessly and authentically infuse all the 'parts' that we are responsible for

chapter two:
about *think!nQ*

> *The first and most important ability you can develop in a flat world is the ability to learn 'how to learn' – to constantly absorb, and teach yourself, new ways of doing old things or new ways of doing new things. That is an ability that every worker should cultivate in an age when parts or all of many jobs are constantly going to be exposed to digitisation, automation, and outsourcing, and where new jobs and whole new industries, will be churned up faster and faster. In such a world, it is not only what you know but how you learn that will set you apart. Because what you know today will be out of date sooner than you think.*
>
> — Thomas Friedman, *The World is Flat*, 2006

The *Clark think!nQ real learning framework* identifies the stages of the natural learning process. Use of this framework empowers students to learn how to learn, independently, through a process that mirrors real life thinking and learning. Used as intended, *think!nQ*, a representation of the *Clark real learning process* (see p. 91), transforms learning from a teacher-directed model to a student-owned responsibility.

Use of the framework also empowers teachers to move the design and delivery of teaching and learning from a 'theme' based, contrived and inauthentic approach, to one that natually infuses transdisciplinary content, thinking, social skills, communication and information technologies.

Key to the framework is the 'ideate' stage (see p. 87). Learning no longer concludes with a student's ability to share, recall, summarise or 'regurgitate' what has been learned. The *Clark think!nQ real learning process* moves learners to a stage of analysis and evaluation so that, ultimately, students 'USE their learning to make a difference in their life or the lives of others'. Learners are invited to develop solutions to problems they have become aware of; to generate recommendations, alternatives and possibilities; to predict the future, evaluate the future and design proactive strategies to own it; to design products ... the *so what* becomes the self-actualisation of the learning. Learning doesn't end with knowing — it ends in action!

In addition to leading learners to USE their knowledge and act on their knowledge, *think!nQ* embeds the thinking process. As a result, use of the model not only teaches a learner how to learn, it actually promotes the learner's *ability* to learn. A student's ability to design, create, ideate and innovate is significantly enhanced as the learner develops deep knowledge and understanding throughout the *Clark think!nQ real learning process*.

> *think!nQ embeds the thinking process. As a result, use of the model not only teaches a learner how to learn, it actually promotes the learner's ability to learn.*

The *think!nQ* framework

On that note, let's take a closer look at the *Clark think!nQ real learning framework* as a model for the design and delivery of authentic teaching and learning. I have included both an 'at a glance' representation as well as a detailed step by step guide for use.

think!nQ — at a glance

Strategic Planning
- follow the *Clark 9 step planning process* (see Section Four, Chapter Two).

Stage 1: Immersion (free immersion)
- immerse learners in the content, concepts, processes and skills; include issues or further aspects which will engage learners both emotionally and cognitively; set up the 'what if challenge' so learners identify a *so what* to pursuing the learning (Note: this is key to the entire framework and learners do not proceed with further stages until a *so what* has been established — how will the learner USE the new learning to make a difference in their life or the lives of others?); the *so what* may be individual or pursued as a class challenge

Stage 2: Brainstorm and Question (brainstorming and wonderings)
- invite learners to brainstorm what they know about the focus challenge/s using a recording tool of their choice
- invite learners to determine what they will need to know; these wonderings may be incorporated into the class 'must do' inquiry question/s if engaging in a whole class inquiry or learners may be provided an opportunity to pursue individual questions alongside the class question/s; ensure that learners consider WHY they wish to investigate their question/s: "How will this new learning make a difference in your life or the lives of others?"; in directing learners in this regard, relevance is promoted and the *so what* is explicitly identified

Note: the questions are strategic and relate directly to the so what established upon the conclusion of immersion. If I want to write a fairytale for children in Africa who have no access to literature, what do I know and what would I need to know to successfully achieve this?

Stage 3: Plan (planning for action)
- share with learners the *thinkbox* or *thinktower* classroom model indicating the skills, tools and strategies that they will be introduced to during the inquiry process; explain that once they develop their understanding of thinking they will use the *thinkbox* or *thinktower* models to plan with you; eventually they will be provided the opportunity to independently plan all of the tools for use in their personal inquiries using the thinking framework of their choice

Stage 4: Investigate.Organise.Internalise (rigorous investigation)
- provide learners with a *planner* that outlines the entire learning journey; all steps should be clearly identified
- provide learners with *criteria* in the format of a rubric (levelled expectations); learners will reference this criteria to self-evaluate prior to outside evaluation
- provide learners with the *learning and thinking tools* associated with each of the areas of *thinkbox* (information, knowledge/comprehension, analysis, evaluation, synthesis); as each tool and/or strategy is used, each should be immediately identified on *thinkbox* and/or *thinktower* as this will assist in making thinking explicit to the learner; the relationship between thinking skills, tools, strategies and learning process will also become

more explicit; informal internalisation time is provided at the end of each learning session; learners are encouraged to record discoveries and wonderings within their learning journals; target teaching is provided as required; regular debrief sessions are conducted to ensure accuracy and completeness of student accessed information

Stage 5: Stop and Think (what do you now know?)

- internalise - invite learners to self-select a strategy and tool for internalisation of newly accessed information; a lack of knowledge, confusion and/or misunderstanding should result in further investigation and/or target teaching before moving forward in the process
- invite learners to self-select a strategy and tool for sharing their comprehension: What do you now know?

Stage 6: Ideate (development of *so what* idea and communication vehicle)

- invite learners to reconsider how they might 'USE their new learning to make a difference in their life or the lives of others'?; learners may continue with their original idea as determined upon the conclusion of the immersion stage; they may make modifications or include additional actions
- invite learners to determine a communication vehicle which will get their idea to an appropriate audience (this may result in an additional inquiry so that learners can generate criteria for their specific communication vehicle)
- direct learners to put their *so what* idea into action

Stage 7: Innovate and Celebrate (celebrate and validate the learning journey)

- direct learners to trial and monitor the results of their *so what*
- invite learners to celebrate the learning journey while waiting to identify if their *so what* idea made the intended difference
- develop and implement a three part celebration that includes:
  — formal sharing
  — informal sharing
  — social time

Stage 8: Evaluate (track thinking and learning process and set goals)

- direct learners to track (underline) the thinking skills, tools and strategies used during the inquiry on their *thinkbox/thinktower* framework
- invite learners to identify the strengths and weaknesses of their thinking tool selections and set goals for improving their thinking during their next inquiry (using the *S.W.SW* tool)
- invite learners to identify the strengths and weaknesses experienced during each stage of the *Clark think!nQ real learning process* (using the *S.W.SW* tool)
- guide learners to set goals for reference during their next inquiry (using the *S.W.SW* tool)

think!nQ – an elaboration

Now that you have seen a snapshot of the process, let's examine each stage in detail. The planning of a *Clark think!nQ* inquiry is a unique process in itself and will be introduced in Section Four, Chapter Two.

We will begin at the immersion stage of the process. You may wish to cross reference your 'at a glance' model, in an effort to better make connections between the two resources.

Stage 1: Immersion

Immersion is a time to 'muddy the learner in muck'. Prior to beginning a new learning focus, teachers often provide learners with initial experiences that 'set the stage' for the learning to come and to promote interest. The principles underlying the immersion stage of the *Clark think!nQ real learning framework* for learning build upon these intentions and extend them. The immersion stage within the *Clark think!nQ real learning process* accomplishes the following outcomes:

Immersion engages the learner cognitively and sets them up with the foundation to ask rich, strategic and personally meaningful questions.

A learner can't know what they don't know! As a result, learners cannot be expected to become excited, curious and interested in that which they know little about, even with the aid of question starters or probes. Quite simply, immersion 'immerses' the learner in new areas of focus in an effort to promote cognitive engagement. Because rich questions require a foundation of knowledge, learners are better able to develop personally meaningful questions as their knowledge base expands.

Immersion models new language, tools, strategies and thinking that learners will later use as they move toward greater independence and self-direction in their learning.

Opportunities are strategically designed by the teacher to embed content, new language, a diversity of thinking tools, strategies and skills. Information organisers will play a critical role in directing the learner toward meaningful discoveries. Strategies and tools which promote analysis, evaluation and synthesis thinking will also be purposefully incorporated into all immersion opportunities. Teachers, and later students, must become literate in selecting, designing and sequencing organisers, and must become well versed in a diversity of critical and creative thinking tools. Independent, self-directed learning requires a significant repertoire of skill sets and literacies. With experience and teacher modelling, learners develop independence and self-direction. It is this ability that will eventually result in the learner designing and owning their own learning.

Immersion promotes the development of deep knowledge and understanding by providing the learner with early finding out and processing experiences.

Deep knowledge and understanding develop over time through repeated engagement in the *Clark real thinking process*. Immersion offers a learner the opportunity to develop increased depth and breadth of understanding as they find out, analyse, evaluate and synthesise newly acquired information through the explicit infusion of thinking tools. By engaging in the immersion stage of learning, the student is prepared for more strategic investigations, and the deep level of analysis, evaluation and synthesis necessary for far transfer.

Immersion promotes the opening of the reticular activation system in the brain which enhances a learner's ability to absorb new learning and make connections.

The brain filters out so much more than it filters in. Pre-visiting new content, language, tools, strategies and skills enables the brain to attend to these more readily when they are addressed again later during strategic learning opportunities.

Immersion engages the learner emotionally, subsequently setting the scene for internally motivated learning.

Teachers often query how they can 'motivate' their learners. Sustained motivation comes from within. As a result, discovering ways to promote 'internal motivation' becomes one of an educator's greatest challenges in the design of effective instruction. Immersion opportunities are designed to highlight issues, or problems or challenges, which encapsulate a diversity of content areas and necessitate the use of a myriad of processes and skill sets. The learning opportunities offered during the immersion stage are not designed to 'teach content and skills', this occurs seamlessly when the opportunities have been created strategically. Instead, this stage in the learning model immerses learners in issues that are developmentally and culturally applicable to them. Immersion attempts to engage the learner emotionally in an issue so that they are eager to learn more about it; keen to find possible solutions; enthusiastic enough to persist when the going gets tough.

The immersion stage of the learning process must result in the learner recognising a greater purpose to pursuing the learning ahead. The *so what* must be explicitly identified by the learner prior to moving on to the next stage of the learning process.

Stage 2: Brainstorm and Question

The brainstorming and question stage follows immersion. The icons are shown side by side, as it is in reflecting on what we know that we naturally consider what we do not know. Learners are invited to brainstorm what they believe they know about the issue or challenge identified in immersion. They also record what they don't know but need to know in order to achieve their *so what*. Questions at this time are not arbitrary, they are strategic. The learner's questions will relate directly to the *so what* action identified and will therefore guide the learners' investigations.

Stage 3: Plan

A planning stage is the next focus for the learner. Effective planning is a critical component of a successful *Clark think!nQ real learning process*. The learner must consider the learning sequence, the thinking tools and strategies that will be used, and the timelines that will be followed.

In a real learning situation, lesson plans are not provided for the learner. In pursuit of learning, the journey, from design to implementation, is predominantly the responsibility of the learner. Because the eventual goal of the *Clark think!nQ real learning process* is student owned learning, it will be the learner who is responsible for planning the *!nQuiry*. Learners will eventually plan the tools that they will use to access new information; the recording tools and strategies they will require; organisers for information management; criteria that will ensure a quality process; as well as the evaluation tools that will assist them in the critical analysis of information and learning effort.

In preparation for student-owned planning, teacher modelling should incorporate a number of components. Teachers should first provide learners with a sequential plan of the entire learning journey. This will ensure that learners know where they are, and where they are going. As learners become familiar with *!nQuiry* as a process, self-direction will become evident as learners follow their plan to move forward independently.

It is also recommended that teachers explicitly name and identify all tools and strategies to be used throughout the *!nQuiry*. This can be easily done by underlining these on the poster sized classroom *thinkbox* or *thinktower* and highlighting this pre-planning for the students to see. In order for learners to one day make tool and strategy choices independently, they must be cognisant of the tools they are using and the rationale behind each selection. Eventually, learners will use the *thinkbox* or *thinktower* frameworks themselves to independently plan the thinking tools they will use for finding out, recording, analysing, evaluating and synthesising their learning.

Stage 4: Investigate.organise.internalise

The investigate.organise.internalise stage invites learners to do just that — investigate their learning while simultaneously managing their information on an organiser which outlines their key focus areas and questions. Learners today have instant access to more information than their ancestors had in a lifetime. A critical aspect of information access is the ability to distinguish between the relevant and irrelevant. Use of a labelled organiser directs the learner and promotes focus on pertinent information only. Further to this, organised information facilitates thinking. With all information readily available in one location, learners are better equipped to analyse and evaluate new information during and following their investigation. Ultimately, this analysis and evaluation will enable the learner to consider how they might USE newly acquired data.

The choice of organiser is eventually that of the learner. Strategic framing and sequencing of organisers ensures a rigorous investigation which meets desired 'endcomes'. In order for learners to eventually own this stage, repeated modelling is required. Learners must be given the opportunity to experience a variety of organisers, framed and sequenced in a diversity of ways.

It is also critical that they are given the opportunity to evaluate the organisers, their framing and sequence. This reflective process will enable them to eventually make organiser-related decisions independently. As a learner's understanding of each organiser develops in terms of general use and in the ways each can be modified, they are better prepared to self-select tools and design the focus sections within the organiser. In the early experiences of inquiry-based learning, a diversity of organisers can be offered to the learner and self-selection promoted. Following this, teacher and learners may co-design organisers; using the modelling opportunity as a segue to learner-owned selection, design and use.

The importance of a well-designed organiser cannot be over-emphasised. It is the organiser that ensures that rigour is maintained throughout the investigation; it is the organiser that ensures that powerful learning outcomes are achieved; it is the organiser that promotes explicit processing through its framing for analytical, evaluative and synthesis thinking; it is the organiser that moves information access from an exercise in learning 'how to research for the purpose of recalling information' to a purposeful, authentic means to an end — finding out so that information can be 'USED to make a difference'.

The 'investigate' aspect of this stage also requires closer consideration. In addition to identifying the resources that will be accessed during the investigation, learners are encouraged to follow the 'resource sequence' as it appears within the stage 'icon'. Interactive, multisensory tools are used to access information before more passive or unisensory tools. Best practice suggests that learners move from the concrete to the abstract. As teachers we talk this talk but plan the multisensory excursion last and access the book or internet first. In the *Clark real learning process,* learners are first invited to interact with their five senses; speak with experts in a face to face interaction, via fax, phone, email or audio/video conference; explore the arts and literature; access dynamic resources such as CD/DVD material and websites. Following these experiences, learners are directed toward less interactive tools such as video or audio; finally print material such as newspapers, magazines, journals and non fiction books are accessed by the learner. Information technologies are seamlessly and purposely infused as learners select and access tools which are necessary to their investigations. Technology upskilling also moves from 'just in case' teaching, to 'just in time' teaching. Learners are motivated to learn new skills and are more likely to retain skill development as a result of the emotional and cognitive engagement associated with purpose and ownership.

The 'internalise' aspect of this stage must also be discussed in order to clarify its purpose and its place in the inquiry process. In an effort to promote deep understanding, learners are consistently directed toward reflection periods as they access and record new discoveries. This ongoing 'find out — lock it in' approach to learning is consistent with the neurological research suggesting a relaxed, reflective state as the optimum for locking new information into the brain. Further to this, analytical and evaluative thinking is promoted and prior learning is built upon.

Stage 5: Stop & think

The stop & think stage invites the learner to reflect and 'take stock' of their learning and the process so far. Learners consider what they now know and evaluate both the quantity and quality of information obtained. This checkpoint may result in the return to prior stages, revisiting the questioning stage; revising their original plan and/or accessing further information. Should learners feel confident and satisfied with their findings, they are directed toward an 'internalisation' time.

Providing a time for learners to reflect on new learning and 'make meaning' is critical in the learners' developmental journey toward more sophisticated thinking. Learners first self-select an internalisation strategy and tool best suited to their personal learning style. It is critical that learners self-select their internalisation strategy and tool as all too often teachers offer group discussion or an alternate 'must do' option which invariably does not cater to the learner's personal learning modality. Options are outlined for reference on *thinkbox* in the knowledge. comprehension section of the framework (see p. 54).

strategies	tools - what is used to meet your strategy
• self talk/visualise/reflect • group talk • writing • visualising • dramatising • manipulating • movement (some learners require physical movement and downtime in order to internalise)	• mind/body • mind/body • pen, pencil, crayons, paper, computer and software • mind/body, camera (still or video), computer and software, paper, pencil, canvas, paintbrush, crayons • mind/body, costumes, props, puppets • manipulatives (models, concrete materials) • mind/body, balls, skipping rope, running shoes

Once learners have reflected using a self-selected strategy and tool, they are invited to Mind Map® their newly acquired information. By engaging in an approach which mirrors the way the brain receives and stores information, further internalisation results, and the ability to make connections and see relationships is enhanced. For information on Mind Maps®, see the works of Tony Buzan as listed in the bibliography.

It is important to note at this point that internalising or processing is actually the act of analysing, evaluating and synthesising. As a result, it is critical to direct learners to use tools that will assist them in engaging in this thinking process. Again, for those teachers using the *thinkbox* or *thinktower* models, learners should reflect on their learning by selecting tools from the analysis, evaluate or synthesis sections of the model.

Once learners have had the opportunity to internalise the learning, make connections and identify relationships, summative assessment, should it be required, is administered. Prior to any 'must do' assessment task, learners are invited to self-select a means of sharing their knowledge and understanding. This inclusionary approach to assessment and evaluation 'walks the talk' of learning styles, Multiple Intelligences Theory and individualisation. Learners can be directed to include specific elements in their sharing but should not be limited to those outlined nor should the learner's vehicle for communication be mandated. Both the 'pick' and 'must do' results are weighted or considered. Should the learner show an understanding of all outcomes on the self-selected assessment tool, but do poorly on the teacher selected task, the former can be revisited by the learner with self-esteem intact. The greater level of confidence and self-esteem experienced by a learner, the greater the potential for growth and development and subsequently, the greater the potential for learning. Learners will be able to address weaknesses when they come to recognise that their difficulty rests not with the learning itself but instead with the assessment approach used. Finally, according to brain researchers such as Caine and Caine, Diamond and Sylwester, to name a few, stress causes a downshifting and subsequent difficulty in the ability to access the neocortex. By enabling a learner to first demonstrate outcomes through a modality of choice, anxiety should be reduced and this should enable learners to better meet their learning potential.

In the traditional education system, this is generally the point where the learning is considered complete and new topics for study are introduced. Learners have researched and proven their understanding through their successful ability to summarise, recall, regurgitate!

The *Clark think!nQ real learning process* challenges this limited, limiting and inauthentic approach to teaching and learning. What is the value in learning for the mere purpose of telling someone else? Where do learners, outside of a school setting, find out for the sole purpose of telling others on tests, through puppet plays or via 'powerpointless' presentations? How many youngsters learned how to ride a bicycle or skateboard so they could tell others about it? How many of us learned to drive, play an instrument or navigate through a software package, simply to tell others what we now know? Individuals may share learning as a natural repercussion of the excitement that came with the new learning experience, but was that the purpose of the learning? This type of learning is not 'real'. Surely, as educators, we can move beyond this inauthentic practice.

Stage 6: Ideate

The ideate stage of the *Clark think!nQ real learning process* is two-fold. The learner develops their *so what* idea as well as a communication vehicle to get the idea to the authentic audience.

The *so what*

"So you know it ... *so what*?!" Learners initiated their learning journey with purpose, a problem or issue they hoped to address. They may still wish to focus on the original issue or may now be aware of further issues or problems that warrant attention. By referencing *thinkbox* in the *so what* section of the model, learners are reminded of the diversity of possible options which will enable them to 'USE their new learning to make a difference in their life or the lives of others'. At this time in their learning journey, the *so what*, conceived during immersion, is brought to the design phase. For example, recommendations are developed; a product is designed; alternatives, plans or solutions are produced. The cyclical nature of learning is reinforced as learners review their information organiser to ensure that they have the data required to develop and act on their *so what* idea. If additional investigation is required, learners move back into the planning and investigate.organise.internalise stages of the model. If further investigation is not necessary, learning is directed toward the design and development of an effective communication vehicle.

The 'communication vehicle'

Once the learner has created their *so what* idea, the learning 'message' becomes apparent. An authentic audience for this message must be considered along with the most effective means of reaching that audience. It is only at this point that the learner considers a communication vehicle.

In the 'real' world of learning, a communication vehicle is not determined until an individual has a message and audience. In contrast to this practice, classroom learning often begins with the learner knowing before the 'research project' begins, that they are eventually going to share or 'regurgitate' their new learning to their teacher and classmates through a 'powerpointless' presentation or a 'diarrhea diorama'.

Because the *Clark think!nQ real learning process* mirrors real learning, a communication vehicle is not selected until the learner has determined their message and audience. Learners do not communicate to their teacher and classmates at the end of a unit for the mere sake of communicating. In *think!nQ*, both the audience and the communication vehicle are authentic. For example, if a learner develops recommendations for water conservation, they must identify their target audience. If the recommendations are for the local community, they may decide to communicate those recommendations through a newspaper editorial. If another learner has pitched their recommendations at the school community, they may decide to share these through the dissemination of posters around school or daily morning announcements. Learners are required to justify their selected communication vehicle based upon their audience and message. In an effort to ensure that the learner develops a 'quality' communication vehicle, the learner should be directed to complete an inquiry into the characteristics of the identified communiqué. What are the characteristics of a great editorial? What are the characteristics of a great poster? Learners may return to the *immersion* stage and move through subsequent stages until they can identify at the *stop & think* stage what they know about the characteristics of their selected communication vehicle. Use of the *thinkitgreat* process will facilitate the independent development of their criteria and should therefore be recommended for use. When the *Clark think!nQ real learning process* is being used at its greatest level of sophistication, support frameworks are provided to assist learners in their decision-making with regard to both their *so what* and communication vehicle. These have been included for your reference in the model provided on the accompanying CD-ROM.

Stage 7: Innovate.celebrate

Innovate

But how do learners know if they have 'made a difference'? Again, concluding the learning at this point would be limiting. The real learning has yet to be realised. The *ideate* stage naturally guides learners to idea generation and design . The *innovate* stage encourages the learner to trial that idea, monitor the impact and outline the results, positive or negative. If no difference has been achieved, was the difficulty in the communiqué or in the *so what* invention? 'Think innovation' is an invitation to go beyond the idea. It's about finding the idea that truly works, the idea that makes that difference!

In order to 'know' whether the idea was successful, learners are required to collect pre and post data. For example, if learners aim to improve the state of water conservation, they first collect baseline data which indicate the current behaviour of their target audience. Once learners share their recommendations, they must collect post data that evidence the behaviours of the target audience following the sharing of their recommendations for change. Learners need to determine whether their recommendations have made a difference. This cannot be achieved without the explicit collection of pre and post data. As a second example, if learners were to develop a plan to improve their learning and decrease stress, video evidence demonstrating their learning prior to the implementation of their plan would be required. Once learners put their plans into action, new video evidence would indicate the effectiveness of the strategies designed. Evaluation, problem solving and goal setting follow.

Celebrate

Celebration validates learning. Regardless of whether 'a difference' was achieved, the process and thinking of *!nQuiry* are celebrated. Learners are invited to plan and implement a 'celebration of learning' that includes a formal and informal sharing opportunity and a social experience.

Formal sharing

In small groups, learners are responsible for formally explaining details about the tools, strategies and processes used during their *think!nQ* learning journey. One group is invited to discuss the specific organisers used to promote information management and analytical thinking; another group shares the diversity of frameworks used, and outlines their role in developing independence, self-direction and quality endcomes; a third group outlines the evaluation tools used to promote judgment and decision-making; and a forth and fifth group share the *thinkbox* and *think!nQ* frameworks respectively, in an effort to help invited guests understand their quest to learn how to think and learn how to learn. Criteria for formal speaking and presenting is generated through the use of the *Clark thinkitgreat process*; and technologies are introduced purposefully as tools to enhance communication. The *thinkitgreat process* should also be used to determine criteria for a great multimedia presentation should this form of communication be incorporated into their formal sharing.

Informal sharing

An informal sharing time provides all learners with the opportunity to celebrate their individual journey with significant others. Learners share their personal organisers, planners, evaluations and, most importantly, *so what* ideas. Criteria for informal communication is generated and used by learners to assist in this skill development. Again, this can be developed through the use of the *thinkitgreat process.*

Social time

A social time provides learners an authentic opportunity to implement a diversity of life skills. Students learn what it means to 'host' a party; they gain experience greeting and seating guests; they learn to make and serve refreshments and clean up responsibly. *Petite!nQuiries* can be introduced at this time to assist learners in not only identifying these discrete skill sets but, more importantly, developing the deep knowledge and understanding necessary for truly effective implementation.

All aspects of the celebration are recorded on video. This enables learners to view their efforts, evaluate and set learning goals for improvement. Parents unable to attend the celebration can access the video at their convenience.

This stage of the learning process provides learners with an opportunity to determine a menu, prepare food and drink, organise space and set timelines. It promotes the development of cross-curricular skills but, most importantly, a strong message is sent ... learning deserves to be celebrated!

Stage 8: Evaluate

The final stage of the *Clark think!nQ real learning process* invites reflection, critical analysis, evaluation and goal setting. In addition to evaluating the *so what* idea and communication vehicle generated during the ideate stage of the framework, the learner is invited to evaluate the learning undergone during each stage of the inquiry process. Thinking is also evaluated as the learner reflects on the tools and strategies used throughout the process. Learners are directed to use the *S.W.SW* evaluation tool when reflecting on product, process and thinking. Learners are encouraged to record a minimum of one strength, one weakness and one *so what* idea in each area. Goals are filed and referenced during the planning of their next *!nQuiry*.

The *Clark think!nQ real learning* model for student use has been included on the CD-ROM. It is recommended that this be provided to your students and used as a 'tracker'. As learners move through each stage of the process, they should indicate completion by highlighting or colouring the icon stage name. The goal of any thinking and learning tool is that one day, it will not be explicitly required. Eventually, the stages of the process will become a natural means of operation. Once internalised, learners will progress through the stages unaided.

The whole

It is my sincere belief that learning *how to learn* is in fact the whole. There is nothing bigger where teaching and learning are concerned. When we teach our kids how to learn all other parts infuse seamlessly. You can't learn without thinking. As a result, thinking is a part of something bigger. You can't learn powerfully without problem solving, decision-making, utlilising time management skills, acting independently and interdependently. You need to self assess and accept that outside assessment is a natural part of the process. Integration occurs naturally in real learning. It is time educators recognised that the only place subjects exist is in school. Real learning engages cross-disciplinary learning. Most critically, real learning holds purpose and relevance for the learner and that purpose is known at the beginning of the process, it is NOT determined at the end. The purpose drives the learning; it drives the need for the knowledge; it drives the need for the processes; it drives the need for the skills. Consequently, purpose must drive the design and delivery of curriculum.

think!nQ™
real learning process

think!nQ framework

lane clark ©

real thinking, real assessment, real technology infusion, real cross curricular integration, real ownership, real self direction, real purpose, real learning

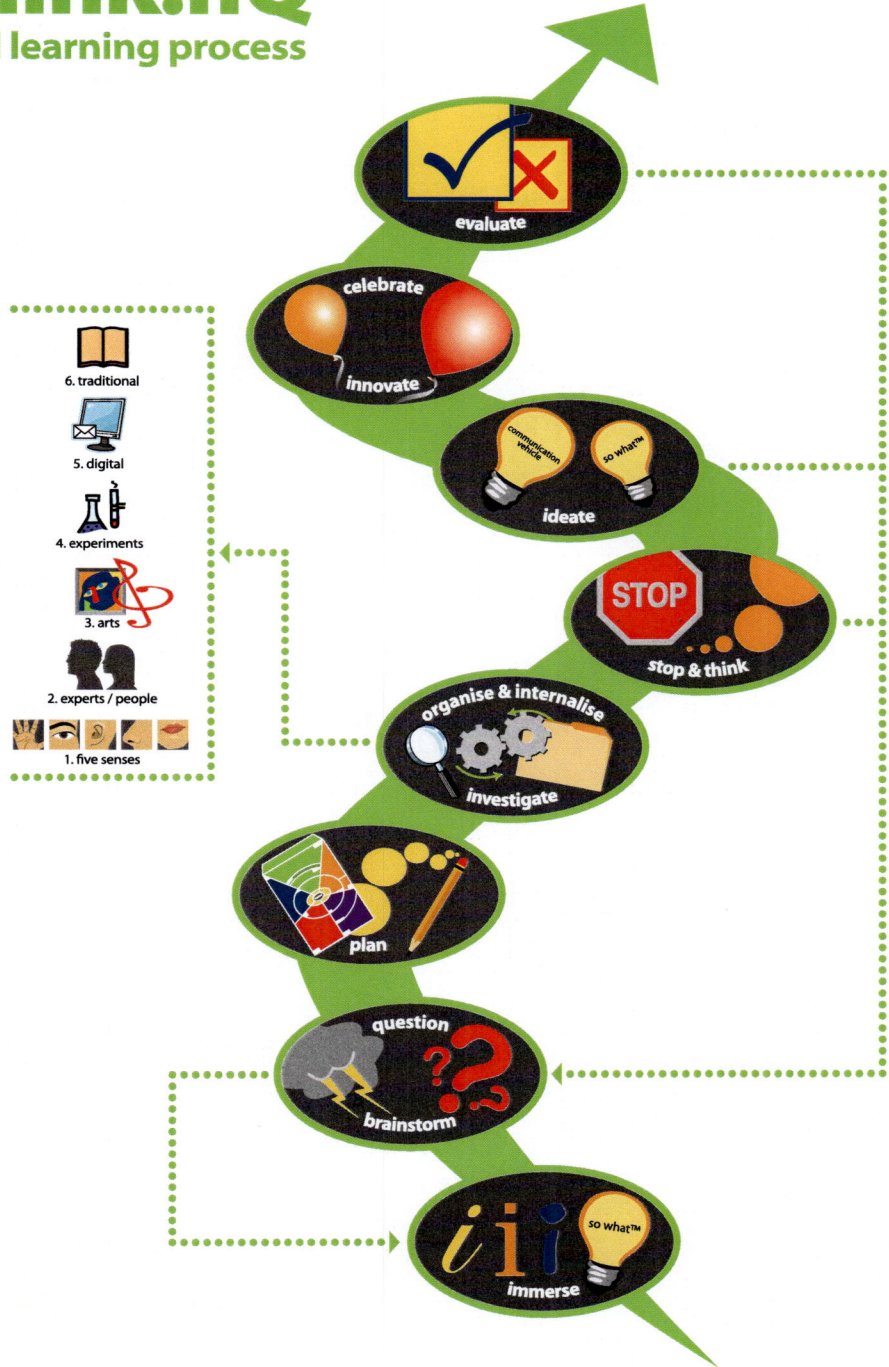

evaluate

celebrate
innovate

communication vehicle
so what™
ideate

STOP
stop & think

6. traditional

5. digital

4. experiments

3. arts

2. experts / people

1. five senses

organise & internalise
investigate

plan

question
?
brainstorm

i i i
so what™
immerse

Action

1. Reflect on the questions provided on page 75. Record your thinking in response to each question. File your responses and date the record. Revisit this task once or twice a year. You will find that as your thinking changes, so too will your practice.

2. Reflect on how you learn and identify each stage of the process.

3. Identify how you currently deliver curriculum.

4. Use a venn diagram to compare and contrast the stages of learning that your students are currently engaging in, with the stages represented in your deconstruction of the learning process.

5. Use the *S.W.SW* tool to outline the strengths and weakness of your current practice. How could you change your design and delivery of curriculum to more comprehensively engage learners in the learning process? Record your ideas in the SW section of your organiser.

Extended Challenge

Complete a *petite!nQuiry* into the characteristics of a diversity of inquiry models for learning. Use the *Clark thinkitgreat process* to determine the characteristics of a GREAT inquiry framework. Remember to use the *thinkchart* organiser. It will direct the rigour and aid in the development of deep knowledge and understanding through its design.

Key to the framework is the 'ideate' stage. Learning no longer concludes with a student's ability to share, recall, summarise or 'regurgitate' what has been learned. The Clark think!nQ real learning process moves learners to a stage of analysis and evaluation so that, ultimately, students 'USE their learning to make a difference in their life or the lives of others'. Learners are invited to develop solutions to problems they have become aware of; to generate recommendations, alternatives and possibilities; to predict the future, evaluate the future and design proactive strategies to own it; to design products ... the so what becomes the self-actualisation of the learning. Learning doesn't end with knowing – it ends in action!

section four

Finally we will consider the natural inter-relationships that exist between the thinking process and learning process. In examining where thinking and learning meet, I will introduce a planning framework that will enable and empower users to design and deliver a comprehensive and authentic curriculum that teaches learners how to think and how to learn.

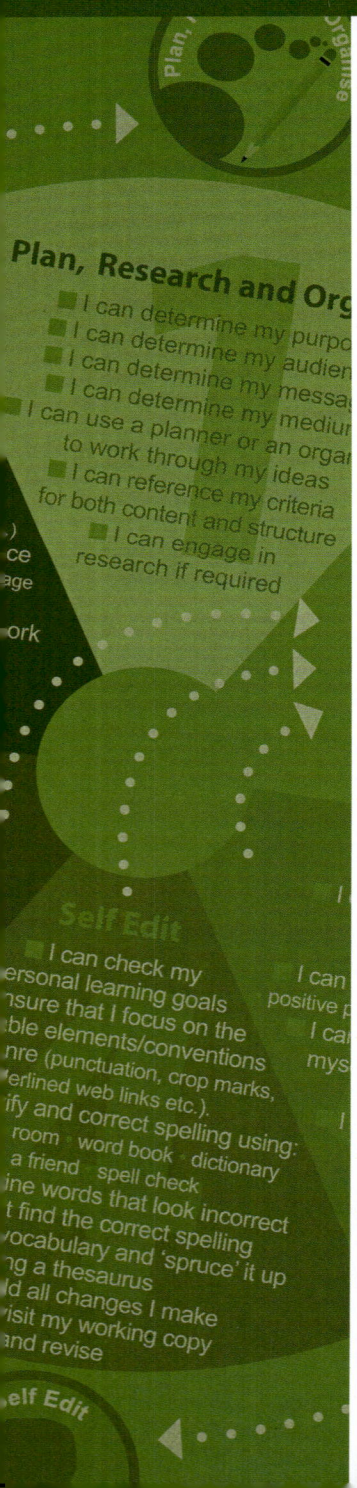

an overview of section four, chapter one: where thinking and learning meet

- The *think!nQ real learning process* guides learners in their learning journey and teaches them how to learn; the *thinkbox* model provides the essential repertoire of tools that promote and enhance the learner's thinking during their learning journey

- The *real thinking process* has been strategically built into the design of the *think!nQ real learning framework*; as a result depth and breadth of thinking are achieved as learners progress through the *think!nQ process*

- The true power of each model rests in its relationship to the other

chapter one:
where thinking and learning meet

Thinking does not occur in a vacuum. It is inextricably entwined within the learning process. For this reason, the *thinkbox/thinktower* thinking frameworks have been designed to work in conjunction with the *think!nQ real learning model*. The *think!nQ* model guides the learner in his learning journey, and teaches him how to learn; and the *thinkbox* model provides the essential repertoire of tools that promote and enhance the learner's thinking during the learning journey. I strongly believe that all learners should know how to learn and how to think. At any time during the learning process, learners should be able to identify the learning tasks at hand; identify the thinking that is required; and then self-select the best thinking tools for the job. They should also be able to frame their organisers, sequence them and layer them as required.

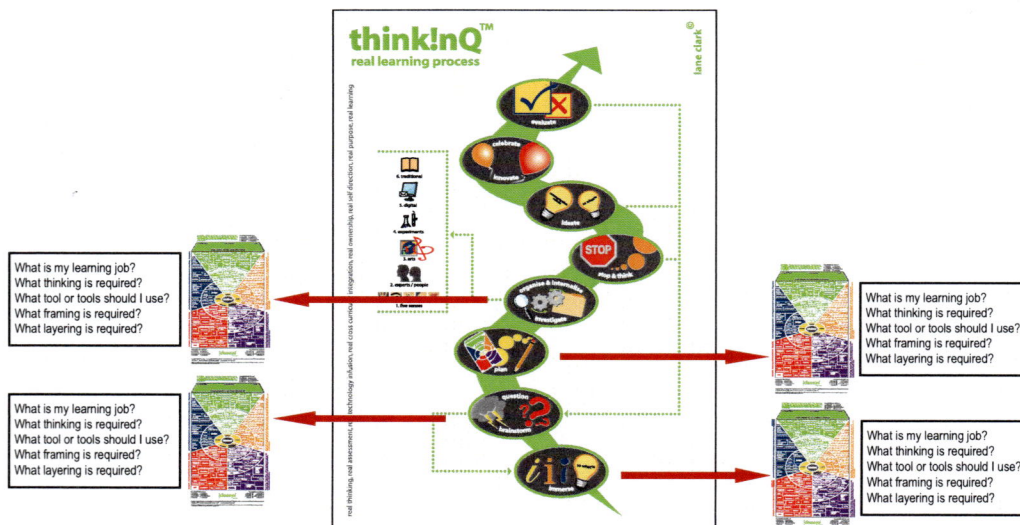

The true power of each model rests in its relationship to the other. While one can clearly see the connections between the *thinkbox* tools and their use within the context of the *think!nQ learning model*, a more critical and significant relationship may be less obvious. The thinking process has been strategically built into the design of the *think!nQ* framework. As a result, depth and breadth of thinking are achieved as learners live the *think!nQ* learning process. Deep learning is realised over time, and the learner's ability to USE his knowledge becomes a reality.

The graphics on the following page will assist in the illustration of this thinking and learning link.

What's the relationship between the *Clark real thinking process* and the *Clark think!nQ real learning process*?

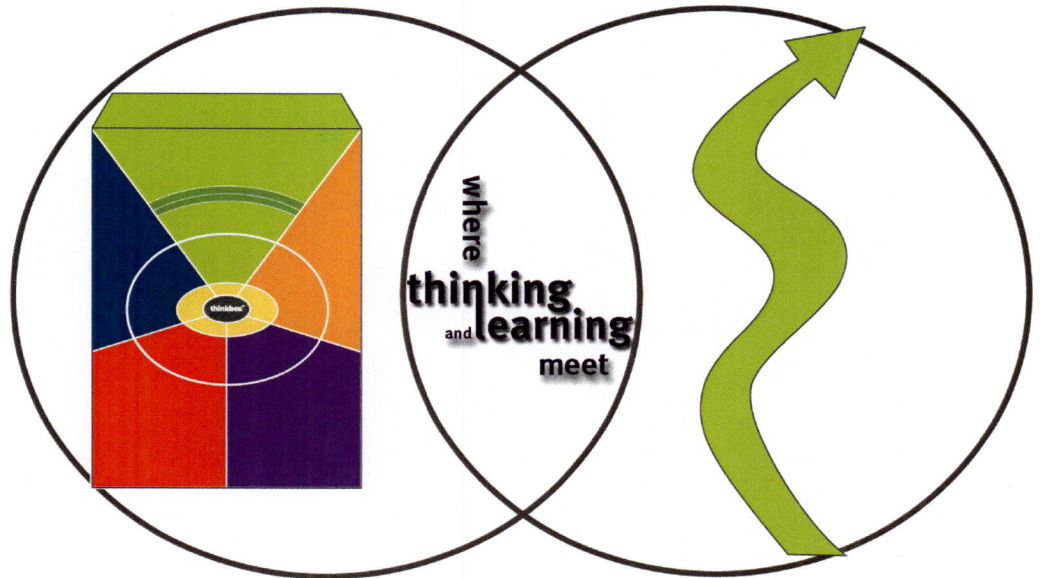

The following figures illustrate the strategic infusion of the *Clark real thinking process* within the design of the *Clark think!nQ real learning process*. As learners move through the inquiry framework, their foundation of information and knowledge.comprehension is built upon. Eventually, far transfer is realised as learners USE their new knowledge to make a difference in their life and the lives of others.

Learners enter a new learning experience with a limited foundation. Depth and breadth must be built upon.

The finding out experience begins during the immersion stage. Thinking tools which promote analysis, evaluation and synthesis are strategically built into the learning opportunities so that early processing is explicitly addressed. Lower level analytical, evaluative and synthesis tools are used as learners are unable to engage in deep processing at this early stage of the journey. The immersion stage should enable the learner to develop two layers of depth and breadth in their foundation as this is required prior to moving into the strategic investigation stage of learning.

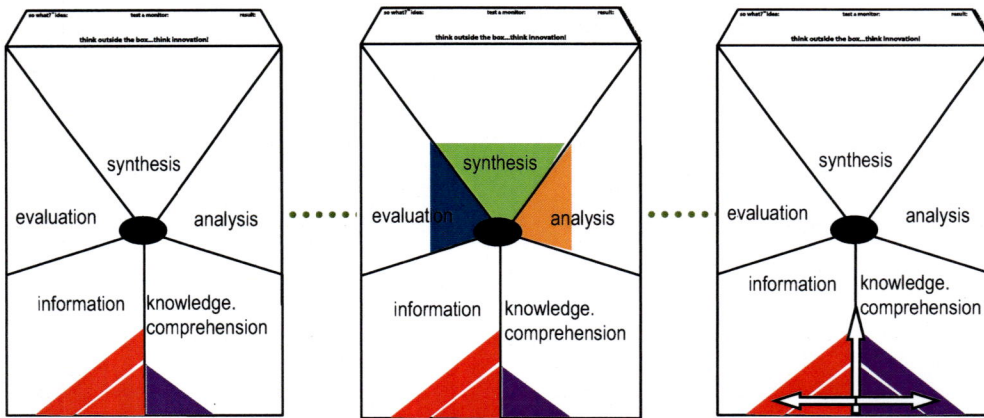

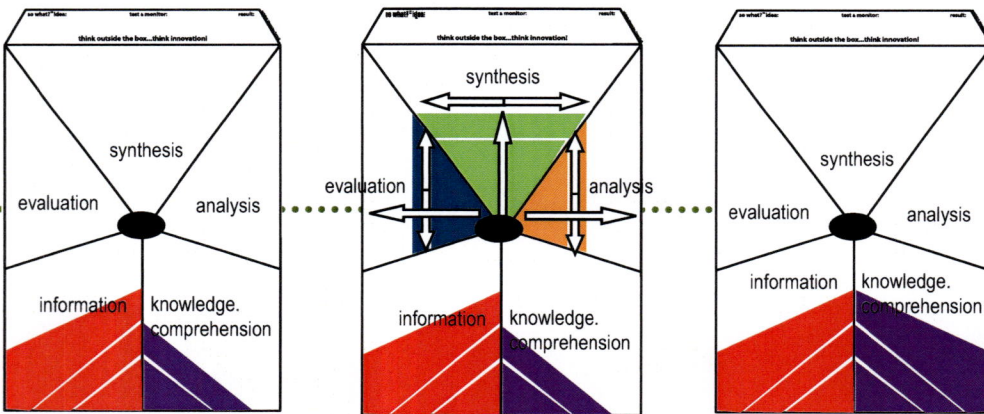

During the strategic investigation phase of the *think!nQ* learning process, real depth and breadth of knowledge and understanding is achieved. Learners have a relatively strong base to build upon. Processing can be strengthened. The learner is capable of analysing, evaluating and synthesising at a much more sophisticated level. The tools provided are more strategic and complex. Upon the conclusion of this learning stage, deep knowledge and understanding has been realised.

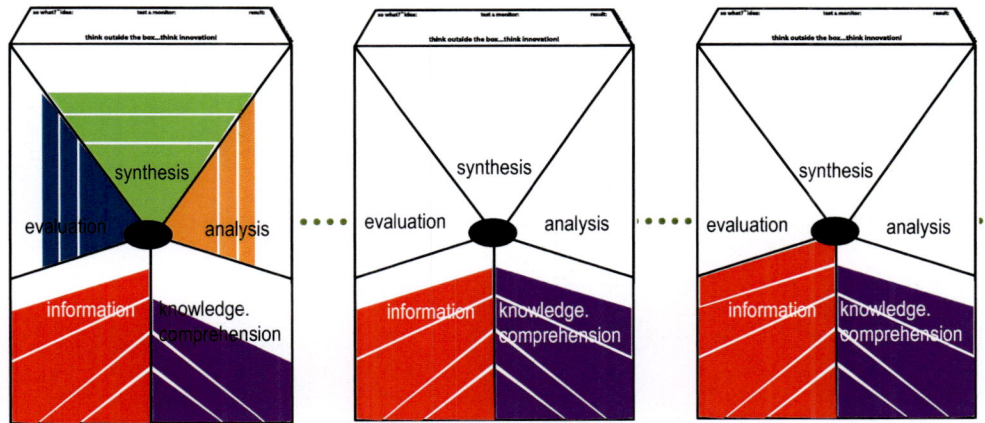

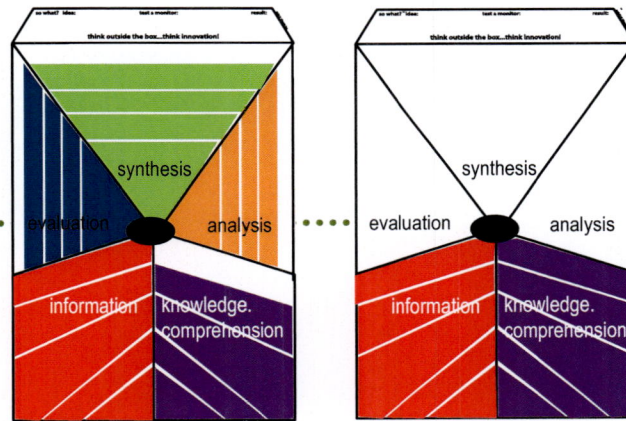

With a solid foundation now in place learners engage in the stop and think stage of the learning process. Should summative assessment be required, it occurs at this time. Learners should be provided with the opportunity to communicate their learning through a modality of choice prior to the mandated mode. While the learner is likely to demonstrate a greater level of knowledge and understanding through their self-selected communication vehicle, the processing over time will enable all learners to experience a greater level of success regardless of the assessment format.

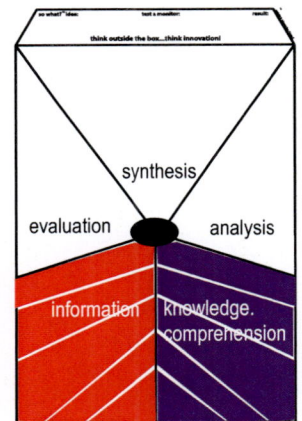

ideate

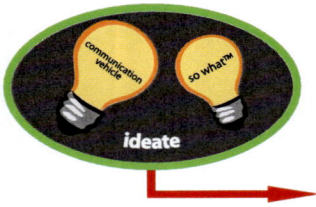

Deep knowledge and understanding has grown over time through a 'process of thinking' and learning. With this new foundation in place, learners can engage in deep analysis and deep evaluation of their new learning. This anchored thinking sets the learner up for high level synthesis or 'far transfer'. At the ideate state of the learning process, learners are invited to analyse and evaluate what they know, and USE it to make a difference in their life and the lives of others.

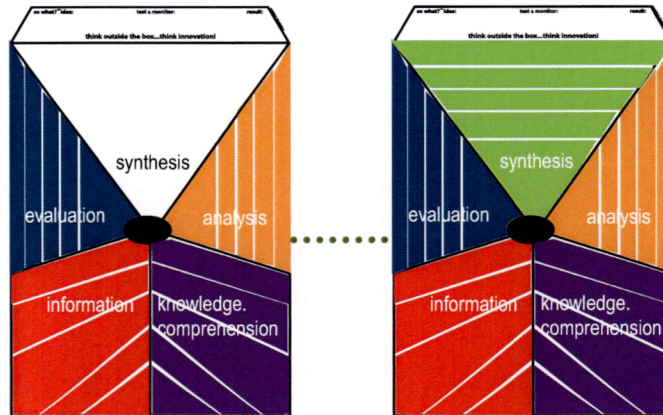

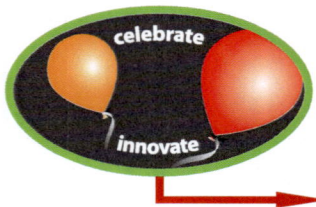

innovate

At the innovate stage of the *think!nQ* learners are invited to put their *so what* idea into action, test and monitor it, and eventually determine whether they did in fact use their new knowledge to make a difference in their life and/ the lives of others.

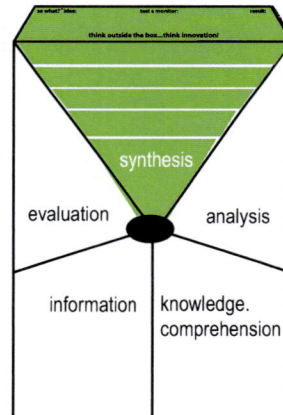

evaluate

The evaluation stage invites learners to reflect upon both their thinking and learning tools, skills and strategies. Thinking and learning goals are set for their next inquiry. The learner is encouraged to ask new questions as the more they know, the more they know they don't know! The finding out experience begins again ... a 'full' *thinkbox* becomes an empty one ... the cycle of thinking and learning is new again.

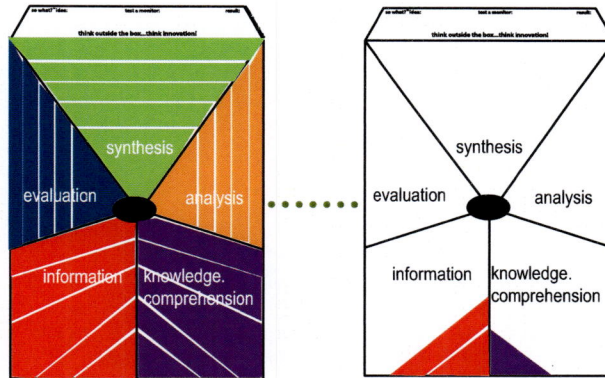

Assessment and evaluation

I have spoken in depth about how the thinking and learning process interrelate, and have outlined a practical means of addressing both processes within the context of curriculum delivery. Before I consider how curriculum planning must change to facilitate this new approach, I must briefly discuss the assessment and evaluation piece of the teaching and learning puzzle.

One of the most significant challenges we face as we design our way forward in this field of teaching and learning is the address of assessment and evaluation. There is curriculum that we are accountable for and outcomes or standards that our learners must achieve. Regardless of its attractiveness or claims, if a pedagogical approach does not explicitly and comprehensively address these areas, it cannot be taken seriously.

You will find within the planning approach provided that curriculum knowledge, skills and processes are addressed explicitly. Further to this, you will see where assessment criteria is built in and how it is built into the planning process. Throughout the planning document, you will also find specific examples of assessment criteria as it relates to the planning sample provided. What you will not find is a step-by-step guide to developing these assessment criteria. While this is a fundamental component of the Clark approach to pedagogical change, the area is simply too vast to address within this book. I have however detailed my thinking and approach to assessment and evaluation within my book, *where thinking, learning and assessment meet* (Hawker Brownlow Education, 2009). It is in understanding where thinking, learning and assessment meet that you will be truly enabled and empowered to initiate and sustain change in your practice.

an overview of section four, chapter two: planning

- The *Clark 9 step planning process* promotes comprehensive, authentic and responsible curriculum and instructional design

- The *Clark real thinking process* and the *Clark real learning process* are about engagement, enablement and empowerment; they are about teaching learners how to think and how to learn; they are about preparing learners for their future, not our past

chapter two:
planning

So how does planning change to meet this approach to the delivery of curriculum that embeds thinking process and learning process seamlessly? How do educators provide an opportunity for kids to learn 'how to learn', promote individual learner interests and foster the development of independence and self-direction while ensuring that specific learning outcomes are achieved? Finding the balance between content knowledge, process and skills, and ensuring that the learning results in an 'end' which is personally relevant to the learner TODAY is perhaps one of an educator's greatest challenges ... the answer lies in your planning.

Below you will find a nine step, 'at a glance' planning guide. Beginning on the next page, I take an elaborated look into each planning stage through the provision of a fairytale example.

The fairytale example used in the planning document was specifically selected because it is a universal concept that should be easily understood by all readers. It is the process that is transferable and therefore it is the process that should be attended to, not the content. While this (fairytale) example is neither complete nor exhaustive, it illustrates the 'at a glance' planning in enough detail to get you started on your journey.

The *Clark 9 step planning process* – 'at a glance'

1. *Start with the end in mind* (Stephen Covey)

   Outline in *specific detail* what you would like the students to **know** and **understand** at the **end** of the learning opportunity. Unpack your outcomes/standards in detail. The more specific the better. The rigour of the learning is identified at this time, as is the thinking. This unpacking will see itself realised within the organiser/s created for the students.

2. Ask Why 5 Deep ...

   Why do my learners need this knowledge and understanding...
   — at this age?
   — at this time in their life?
   — at this developmental level?
   — in this community?
   — in this culture?

   How could my learners USE this knowledge and understanding to make a difference in their life or the lives of others TODAY?

3. Identify the *so what* possibilities.

   Could my learners develop solutions to problems they become aware of; alternatives; new possibilities; recommendations; future predictions; new products?

   Pick one or two to drive the *!nQuiry*.

4. Revisit the curriculum documents for additional cross-curricular knowledge that *underpins* the *so what*

5. Design the main organisers for the investigate.organise.internalise stage of the learning process; develop the corresponding **knowledge criteria for investigating** (investigate stage) and the **knowledge criteria for producing** (ideate stage).

6. Identify the cross-curricular processes that your learners will use as they move through all stages of the learning process (i.e. *thinkitgreat* process, *sciencethink*, *techthink*, *jigsaw cooperative group* framework, *publisher's process*); develop the **process criteria** for each framework/process required.

7. Identify the cross-curricular skills that the learners will require as they move through all stages of their *!nQuiry* (i.e. reading skills, writing skills, word processing skills, illustrating skills, team skills, collecting, representing and analysing data skills); develop the corresponding cross-curricular **skills criteria.**

8. Develop 'immersion' opportunities; these incorporate the knowledge, processes and skills of the entire inquiry and should assist learners in achieving '2 layers deep' in their foundational knowledge; ensure that the *so what* driving the learning is explicitly designed into at least one immersion opportunity; strategically design learning to cognitively and emotionally engage the learner; collect baseline data for knowledge and skills.

9. Name the unit OR preferably invite learners to name it after they have completed the immersion experience and identified the *so what* that will drive their *!nQuiry*.

The Clark 9 step planning process – 'elaborated'

I have said this before but I MUST say it again ... Start with the end in mind! If you are serious about real learning, real thinking and real assessment, the planning scheme outlined below will guide you in your change journey. The sequence challenges the general planning approach which more often than not, entails the consideration of broad outcomes, followed by a hasty development of 'activities' or lesson plans. As indicated below, 'activities' are NOT considered until much later in the planning phase. The first important priority is identifying the rigour and purpose of the learning.

Step 1: What do I want my learners to know and understand at the end of the *!nQuiry*?

I recommend that when possible, you begin with the knowledge areas of the curriculum. Curriculum documents generally embed knowledge, process and skills outcomes. Recognising this, some disciplines tend to have a naturally heavy focus on content while others are more skills based. Knowledge heavy areas include: science, humanities/society and the environment, and health. The skills based disciplines such as English, maths and art cannot be neglected as skills are required in all learning. Consequently these disciplines will be infused later in the planning.

If you are a subject specific teacher, begin with the understandings or knowledge components inherent within your specific discipline documents. You too will address the skills within your discipline later in the planning process.

Content (knowledge/understanding)
What is a fairytale? Be specific! If you would like your learners to know what a fairytale is then you MUST be able to outline the characteristics yourself I want my learners to know the following: • non-specific opening   (one day; once upon a time; long long ago etc.) • past tense • magic • abuse • villain — the baddy — hurts victim — loses at end • victim — character with the hurt heart • hero — the goody — saves victim • problem — something that goes wrong • complication — the solution that doesn't work • resolution — the solution that works and solves the problem • happy ending — the villain loses; the victim is OK

Note: determine and outline specifically the depth of knowledge required for your learners ... What more should learners know about character at this time?
- *age*
- *ethnicity*
- *gender*
- *socioeconomic background*
Are these outcomes appropriate for all learners or should this be addressed as an extension in the criteria provided?

Step 2: Ask Why 5 Deep ...

Once you have specifically outlined your curriculum outcomes/standards, it is important to justify those outcomes in relation to your learners. I am not referring to the obvious... "because they are in the curriculum" or "we always do this unit in week one of term two" or "this is the unit my team has chosen to do". The justification I am asking you to consider goes much deeper than that ...

In the *Clark think!nQ* inquiry framework, learners do not engage in their learning so they can know it ... they engage in their learning so that they can USE it to make a difference in their life. Only when learning is used is it truly relevant. *Clark think!nQ real learning* moves learning beyond interesting to relevant! When kids USE their learning, and it is relevant to the learner, learning is much more likely to be retained in long term memory.

Challenge (WHY?)
Why do my learners require these outcomes at this time? Why at this age? Why at this developmental level? Why in this culture? Why in this community? How can my learners USE this knowledge to make a difference in their life and/or the lives of others today?

Step 3: Determine the *so what* possibilities that will drive the *!nQuiry*

In the fairytale example outlined, I struggled to determine a meaningful *so what* or way in which they could USE their learning about the characteristics of fairytales to make a difference in their life or the lives of others. After digging deeper into relevant possibilities, I decided that 'fairytales' per se, were less important to my learners than a general love and appreciation of literature; and the ability to read stories whenever they wanted to. I questioned my learners' genuine valuing of literature and realised that this could be the driving force behind my 'fairytale' focus, recognising that any genre would also enable me to meet this end goal.

What if I could immerse my learners in a culture of children who did not have the luxury of books to read on demand? What if I could immerse my learners in a school community where resources were extremely limited? Perhaps this would motivate my learners to want to learn how to write books for these children and consequently want to learn more about the children and their culture in general so that they might successfully create books which appeal to their audience.

It should be noted that I do have a topic. Although I have to meet outcomes regarding the elements of this genre, at this time I have simply unpacked those outcomes. I have not 'named' the unit, nor have I created any activities or lesson plans. Outcomes can be met through a wide variety of topic choices. NEVER choose a topic first; simply record outcomes and allow the topic to evolve over time.

Step 4: Consider further underpinning knowledge and understanding

Planning should be a back and forth exercise. As the *so what* possibilities are determined, the need for further knowledge and understandings become apparent. For example, if learners are to write books which cater to their audience, it is necessary for them to hold an understanding of the culture of that audience.

Further Knowledge and Understandings

What is culture?

I want my learners to know the following:
- what do the people look like? (eye, hair, skin, colour)
- what do they do?
  — work
  — play
  — education
- how do they live?
  — food
  — clothing
  — shelter
- what is their environment like?
  — plants
  — animals
  — land features
- what are their beliefs?
- what are their celebrations?
- how do they communicate?
  — language
  — visual images
  — dance
  — music

In order to successfully meet the *so what* challenge, which in this example involved the writing of literature for a group of less fortunate learners, further outcomes must also be addressed. In addition to learning about the culture of their audience, learners should know the component parts that make up the structure of a book. Because their audience will have English as a second language, learners need to know the characteristics of great illustrations so that their images can support the written text.

When revisiting the curriculum at this point in the planning process, the focus is on the disciplines that naturally underpin the realisation of the *so what* idea. Integration is thus authentic, powerful and critical. This is in contrast to thematic teaching which is characterised by forced connections.

Step 5: Design the organisers for use during the investigate.organise.internalise stage of the *!nQuiry*

Once the *so what* has been identified and the related cross-curricular content knowledge 'unpacked', the main organisers for the *!nQuiry* can be developed along with the corresponding knowledge criteria for investigation. If the outcomes have been outlined in detail, the rigour will be available for placement in the 'left hand column' of your *thinkchart* organisers. The content knowledge criteria for investigating is also designed at this time. This criteria will allow learners to engage in the investigation at a level of depth and breadth commensurate with their individual ability levels. Provided it is not overwhelming for your learners, the organiser is designed to meet the 'above expected' level of criteria. In doing this, learners are not limited in the outcomes attained during the investigation; and they are guided to the highest level of achievement. Learners who do not complete all sections of the organiser will find that they have met the criteria at a lesser level, which is of course a perfectly acceptable alternative. Because the *so what* has been established, knowledge criteria for producing can also be designed along with the corresponding planners. See accompanying CDROM for A4, digital examples of all organisers, planners and associated knowledge criteria for investigating and producing. (For more information on criteria based assessment and its relationship to the design and delivery of *think!nQ inquiry*, contact office@laneclark.ca).

An example of a main organiser and corresponding criteria; as well as a planner and its corresponding criteria, have both been provided for your reference on the following pages.

fairytale organiser (note: the left hand column corresponds to the desired 'end' knowledge or content; empty sections are included to enable learners to identify additional elements)

Subsequent organisers are also developed (e.g. venn diagrams, cross classification charts for cross checking, if the *thinkitgreat* framework is required in the investigation.)

The example below represents the way in which criteria can be developed to guide learners to varying levels of inquiry investigation. As indicated on page 107, while all learners would receive the same information organiser, they are invited to meet the learning expectations at a level commensurate with their ability. Note that the rubric has been written using the Clark 'criteria for criteria'. It must be in 'kid speak', 'realistic', 'measurable', 'observable' and 'specific'. There is absolutely no room for subjectivity if criteria is to be effectively used by learners and teachers.

thinkchart™ - investigating fairytales criteria lane clark ©

☐ identify the following in the 'Physical' section of the organiser

Beginning Words Once upon a time...

victim villain hero

problem resolution

magic abuse

Ending Words ...happily ever after.

☐ identify the cause OR effect (1/2, 0.50, 50%)

Cause - why would the author choose this?

Effect - what is the impact on the reader?

☐ identify the setting OR plot (1/2, 0.50, 50%)

setting plot

☐ identify the cause AND effect (2/2, 1.0, 100%)

☐ identify the setting OR plot (1/2, 0.50, 50%)

thinkchart™ - investigating fairytales criteria lane clark ©

☐ identify the following in the 'Physical' section of the organiser

Beginning Words Once upon a time...

victim villain hero

problem resolution

magic abuse

Ending Words ...happily ever after.

☐ identify the cause AND effect (1/2, 0.50, 50%)

Cause - why would the author choose this?

Effect - what is the impact on the reader?

☐ identify the setting AND plot (1/2, 0.50, 50%)

setting plot

The more sophisticated the desired 'end' knowledge, the more sophisticated the design of the organiser. The example below illustrates an organiser which has been reframed to enhance student learning during the inquiry. Could you create criteria in a rubric format which would enable learners to meet this investigation at a diversity of levels?

fairytale organiser (note: the left hand column has been modified to include greater breadth and depth of understanding; organiser #1 would attach to organiser #2 at the perforated line.

Characteristics / Diversity	P physical	B cause why? / effect so what? behavioural	E setting environmental plot	S strengths	W weaknesses	SW so what ideas
Beginning Words *Once upon a time...*		C E	o—o—o			
Beginning Weather		C E	o—o—o			
Beginning Natural Place		C E	o—o—o			
Beginning Dwelling		C E	o—o—o			
Beginning Characters		C E	o—o—o			
Problem		C E	o—o—o			
Complication		C E	o—o—o			
Resolution		C E	o—o—o			
Magic		C E	o—o—o			
Abuse		C E	o—o—o			
Ending Weather		C E	o—o—o			
Ending Natural Place		C E	o—o—o			
Ending Dwelling		C E	o—o—o			
Ending Characters		C E	o—o—o			
Ending Words *...? apply ever after*		C E	o—o—o			

Characteristics / Diversity		P physical	B cause why? / effect so what? behavioural	E setting environmental plot	S strengths	W weaknesses	SW so what ideas
Villain	Age		C E	o—o—o			
	Ethnicity		C E	o—o—o			
	Gender		C E	o—o—o			
	Socioeconomic Status		C E	o—o—o			
	Action		C E	o—o—o			
Victim	Age		C E	o—o—o			
	Ethnicity		C E	o—o—o			
	Gender		C E	o—o—o			
	Socioeconomic Status		C E	o—o—o			
	Action		C E	o—o—o			
Hero	Age		C E	o—o—o			
	Ethnicity		C E	o—o—o			
	Gender		C E	o—o—o			
	Socioeconomic Status		C E	o—o—o			
	Action		C E	o—o—o			

As outlined earlier, it is at this stage of the planning process that all organisers for the investigate.organise.internalise stage of the inquiry are designed. The *thinkcharts* overleaf will assist learners in their investigations into culture and the structure of books.

investigating the culture of children in africa - criteria

beginning to develop	at expected	above expected
I can identify all components in the 'Physical' section of my *thinkchart*	I can identify all components in the 'Physical' section of my *thinkchart*	I can identify all components in the 'Physical' section of my *thinkchart*
I can identify the cause of 7 of the 16 components from the designer's viewpoint	I can identify the cause of 8-10 of the 16 components from the designer's viewpoint	I can identify the cause of 11-16 of the 16 components from the designer's viewpoint
I can outline 5–8 ideas for including the culture of my audience into my story	I can outline 9-10 ideas for including the culture of my audience into my story	I can outline more than 10 ideas for including the culture of my audience ... ...

culture organiser
(if learners are to write literature for children in Africa, it is critical that they learn about African culture so that their books are culturally sensitive and appealing.)

characteristics / diversity	P physical — what do you see?	WHY? cause? WHY? B behavioural WHY? WHY?	SW so what idea for including culture in my fairytale
People — skin		c	
hair		c	
eyes		c	
language		c	
values/beliefs		c	
Lifestyle — work		c	
play		c	
food			
celebrations			
Environment — plants			
animals			
land features			
weather			
Arts			
Sport			

© Lane Clark

investigating the structure of a book - criteria

beginning to develop	at expected	above expected
I can identify all components in the 'Physical' section of my *thinkchart*	I can identify all components in the 'Physical' section of my *thinkchart*	I can identify all components in the 'Physical' section of my *thinkchart*
I can identify the cause of 9 of the 19 components from the designer's viewpoint	I can identify the cause of 10-14 of the 19 components from the designer's viewpoint	I can identify the cause of 15-19 of the 19 components from the designer's viewpoint
I can outline 20 of the 57 S. W. SW possibilities	I can outline 21–30 of the 57 S. W. SW possibilities	I can outline 30 or more of the 57 S. W. SW possibilities

book structure organiser
(in order to produce a quality book structure, learners must investigate a diversity of book structures)

Note: further organisers would be required in this sample *!nQuiry*; these would include a thinkchart to investigate the stages of the publisher's cycle and a *thinkchart* to investigate the characteristics of quality illustrations

What are the characteristics of the structure of a book?

* thinkchart™ & S.W.SW™ copyright lane clark

Characteristics / Diversity	P physical	cause why? OPV (designer) B behavioural	S strengths of the structure of the book	W weaknesses of the structure of the book	SW so what™ ideas for the structure of my book
purpose		C			
audience		C			
size		C			
shape		C			
material/s		C			
# of pages		C			
interactivity		C			
attachments		C			
special effects		C			
technique/s		C			
tools		C			
page layout		C			
repetition		C			
text — size		C			
colour		C			
location		C			
images — size		C			
colour		C			
location		C			

* thinkchart™ & S.W.SW™ copyright lane clark
thinkchart™

In this specific *!nQuiry* sample, learners will eventually produce a fairytale book for children in an African community who do not have access to literature. The criteria for the end of unit 'producing' and the corresponding planners are designed at this time in the planning process.

fairytale planner

1

Beginning Words... Once upon a time...

Beginning Weather...

Cause - why did it happen?   Problem   oops!

draw a picture of the problem

☐ I included abuse   ☐ baddy hurts victim

My Fairytale Criteria

⭐   ⭐⭐   ⭐⭐⭐

☐ Include beginning words
non specific
set in past

☐ Include characters
☐ a victim who gets hurt by
the villain

☐ Include a problem with abuse

☐ Include a resolution with magic

☐ Include a happy ending

☐ Include beginning words
non specific
set in past

☐ Include characters
☐ a victim who gets hurt by
the villain
☐ a villain who hurts the victim
and loses at the end
☐ a hero who saves the victim

☐ Justify your characters **WHY?**
why did you choose that victim?
why that villain?
why that hero?

☐ Include a problem with abuse

☐ Include a resolution with magic

☐ Include a happy ending

☐ Include beginning words
non specific
set in past

☐ Include characters
☐ a victim who gets hurt by
the villain
☐ a villain who hurts the victim
and loses at the end
☐ a hero who saves the victim

☐ Justify your characters **WHY?**
why did you choose that victim?
why that villain?
why that hero?

☐ Include a problem with abuse

☐ Justify the problem you chose **WHY?**

☐ Include a resolution with magic

☐ Include a happy ending

2 Cause - why did it happen?   Solution

draw a picture of the solution

☐ I included magic   ☐ hero save

3 Characters
draw a picture of the characters

Victim gets hurt   Villain baddy   Hero goody

Ending Words... ...happily ever after.   End

Action: How does the victim get hurt?
What does the victim do about it?

Action: What does the villain do to the victim?

Action: How does the hero save the victim?

criteria for producing a fairytale
and corresponding criteria

(further criteria would be required for
producing at the 'ideate' stage of the
!nQuiry; in addition to providing learners
criteria for the fairytale, learners would
require criteria for the structure of their
book, their illustrations, their use of the
publisher's process, their use of the
technology process, and the embedding
of culture into their story)

Step 6: Plan all cross-curricular processes

Step 7: Plan all associated cross-curricular skills

The *so what* drives all further planning. It is only now that I can plan the processes and skills to be addressed in the *!nQuiry* because it is only now that I know what processes and skills my learners will need to meet their *so what* challenge. Processes are planned first as they will dictate the need for specific skills.

"I am writing for a public audience, therefore to ensure quality, I will need to use the publisher's process ... the publisher's process directs me to self edit my work for conventions, spelling and grammar during the self edit stage, therefore I will need to accurately use paragraphs, full stops and capitals. I will need to develop my skills in each of these areas."

I hope you can see that EVERYTHING begins with a purpose that is authentic! The knowledge and understandings lead to the *so what*, which naturally infuses specific processes and skills. Let's take a closer look at what might be included within this 'fairytale' example.

processes or frameworks	skills

I will need to introduce the following processes/frameworks:

The *techthink* Technology Process: In order to guide my learners so that they produce a quality product, which in this case is a book, they will need to use the techthink process (briefing, ideating, prototyping, producing). I will also need to develop specific process criteria to guide them in their achievement at each stage.

The *sciencethink* Scientific Method: To assist my learners in conducting a quality investigation during the 'investigate. organise.internalise' stage of their *think!nQ* inquiry, I will need to provide them with the *sciencethink* process (plan, conduct, process, evaluate, communicate). I will also need to develop specific process criteria to guide them in their achievement at each stage.

The *thinkitgreat* Process: In order to responsibly and rigorously identify the characteristics of a fairytale; illustrations, the structure of a book and culture, my learners will need to follow the *thinkitgreat* process (investigate, hypothesise, test, conclude, evaluate). I will also need to develop specific process criteria to guide them in their achievement at each stage.

The *authorthink* Process: Quality publishing can be promoted through the use of a publisher's process. To assist my learners in publishing both a quality fairytale and a quality communication vehicle, I will provide them with the *authorthink* process (plan and organise, working copy, *authorcircle*, self-edit, outside edit, evaluate. publish.celebrate). I will also need to develop specific process criteria to guide them in their achievement at each stage.

The *jigsaw* Cooperative Group Learning Process: In order to expedite the inquiry into multiple fairytale examples; book structure examples; and illustration examples, the jigsaw cooperative group process will be used for all three petite-*!nQuiries*. (One expert group will investigate one example; a second expert group will investigate a second example; experts from each group will pair up to conduct their venn diagram comparative analysis; the hypothesis determined within the midsection of the venn will then be compared with the data found from three further expert groups who have all investigated their own samples; a conclusion outlining viable characteristics will then be determined).

NOTE: The ultimate goal of think!nQ inquiry is independent, student led inquiry, where learners self-select their inquiry focus; select, frame and sequence their organisers; and identify and use the processes required to get their job done. All tools and processes must be explicitly named and provided to learners during this time of teacher ownership and modelling. Criteria, which corresponds to each process, should be developed and used by your learners. When creating rubrics in this regard, focus first on the independent use of each model. Once independence has been achieved, specific expectations for each stage of a process should be built in to achieve 'quality'

Specific skills are targeted depending on learner needs and curriculum needs. All inherent skills do not become a focus ... pick your fights! The criteria is developed as the skills are documented so that assessment and evaluation is NOT an add on but instead infused seamlessly into the learning opportunity. Because the skills are genuinely a part of the learning, the targeted skills are learned within an authentic context. Please note that although the criteria is outlined, it must be negotiated with your learners and may therefore change. Criteria should be developed from baseline data so that it is truly reflective of your learners' developmental needs.

Skills for the *authorthink publisher's process*

Grammar/Spelling/Punctuation

(needed during the working copy and self editing stage of *authorthink*)

criteria:

  beginning to develop:
- I use full stops, capitals for sentences, commas for a pause
- I use words 'up' in the room as a spelling strategy

  at expected level:
- I use question marks, exclamation marks, and experiment with quotation marks and paragraphs
- I use words 'up' in the room, word book, and friends, as spelling strategies

  above expected level:
- I use quotation marks and paragraphs accurately
- I use words 'up' in the room, word book friends and a dictionary, as spelling strategies

ICT Development — Word Processing

(needed during the working copy and self editing stages of *authorthink*)

criteria:

  beginning to develop:
- I use Office WP to input and delete

  at expected level:
- I use Office WP to input, delete, move text, utilise spell check; manipulate font type and size
- I can justify less than 100% of choices

  above expected level
- I use Office WP to input, delete, move text, utilise spell check, manipulate font type and size; manipulate font style (bold and italicise) and input graphics
- I can justify all choices

NOTE: a wide variety of further skills could also be targeted as desired.

At this point in the planning process ...

1) the curriculum has been 'unpacked' for content knowledge, and its rigour has been detailed

2) you have questioned the purpose of the content knowledge in relation to your learners today

3) you have determined a *so what* possibility or a number of possibilities

4) you have revisited your curriculum for cross-curricular content knowledge connections

5) you have designed your main organisers for the investigate.organise.internalise stage of *think!nQ*, along with the associated content knowledge criteria for investigating; you have developed your planners for the 'ideate' stage of think!nQ, along with the associated content knowledge criteria for producing

6) you have outlined the processes to be used in the *!nQuiry* and have developed your process criteria

7) you have outlined the cross-curricular skills to be addressed in the !nQuiry and have developed all associated skills criteria.

Step 8: Design the immersion opportunities

It is now time to design the immersion opportunities which will hook your kids cognitively and more importantly emotionally. The immersion stage of the model is planned by the teacher and is clear in its objectives. It should be noted that although the immersion stage is the first stage lived by learners in the *think!nQ* framework, it is almost the last stage planned by the teacher. Because the immersion stage 'immerses' learners in the knowledge processes and skills of the inquiry; because immersion is used to collect baseline data; and because it embeds the *so what* for identification by the learners, all other aspects of your planning must be outlined before this stage can be strategically addressed.

When planning your immersion opportunities, you must ensure that each one is purposeful. You are not designing activities for the sake of activities. As you design each immersion opportunity, identify its purpose as well as the specific outcomes that will be addressed in each. If the immersion centre is meant to introduce knowledge, then this should be outlined; if it is meant to engage the learner emotionally and share the *so what* possibilities, then this should be documented. Each immersion centre should offer learners an organiser to direct them in their discoveries and thinking. Remember, when you find out, processing naturally occurs. By incorporating tools for analysis, evaluation and synthesis into this early finding out experience, you will support the learner's ability to process. Consequently you will promote the development of knowledge and understanding. This base will be built upon during the investigate.internalise.organise stage of the learning model.

Let's take a closer look at what an immersion opportunity might look like ...

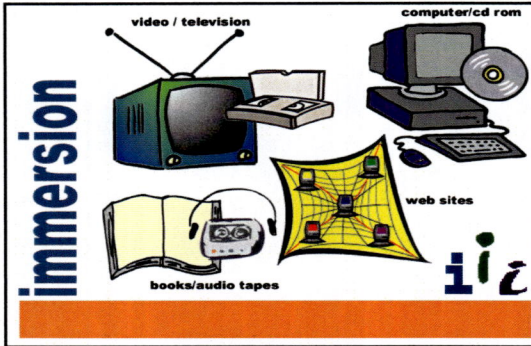

5 centres - using a variety of mediums to share a variety of fairytales; include one or two fairytales that are culturally insensitive to learners (e.g. animals, flora, fauna or languages that are unknown to them)

Purpose: to engage learners in content; to hook them into fairytales; to introduce learners to the idea that they need to keep the intended audience in mind when producing for others - this will set learners up to 'want to' know more about the culture of the kids they are writing for; and 'want to' ensure that their story meets audience need; to introduce learners to a diversity of mediums to learn through; to cater to multiple modalities.

Note: one organiser per fairytale investigation

1 centre - expert author and publisher

Purpose: to introduce learners to aspects of story writing that might otherwise be missed; learners are provided the opportunity to chat with the experts; they are immersed in the need to use a publisher's process if they wish to produce 'quality'; they are immersed in the thinking required when making decisions around character, setting and plot.

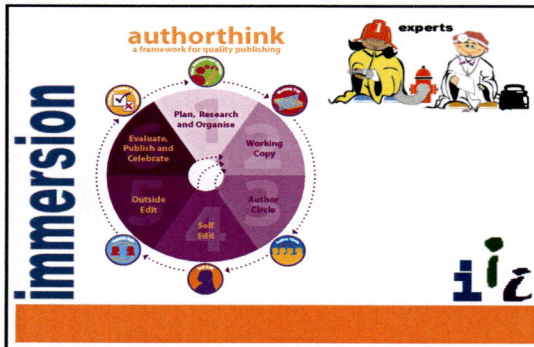

Note: A number of further immersion centres would be provided to further engage learners cognitively and emotionally in focus areas which will be more strategically addressed during the 'investigate.organise.internalise' stage of the *think!nQ process*.

A centre which immerses learners in a diversity of book structures (i.e. big books, novels, picture books, ring bound, stapled, glue bound, stitch bound, card paper, coloured paper, pop-up books, slide books, peek-a-boo books etc.). An illustration centre would be offered to immerse learners in a diversity of illustrators, their techniques and tools.

Exploration in these centres explicitly develops awareness, encouraging questions and the development of opinions. Most importantly, these immersion opportunities promote the development of beginning ideas for their own creations. As with all immersion centres, an organiser would be provided to direct learners loosely in their discoveries and thinking. Remember, deep knowledge and understanding develops over time when the thinking process is infused into the overall design of the learning opportunity. The immersion organiser needs to engage analysis, evaluation and synthesis thinking in order to achieve this result.

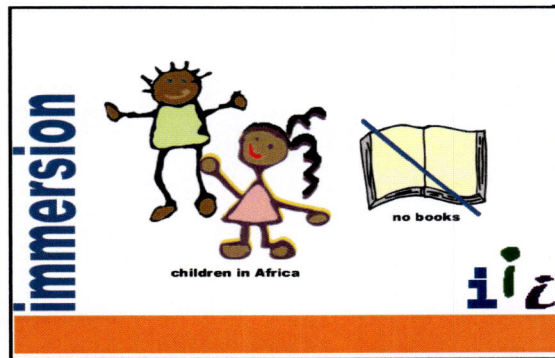

1 centre - expert guest in from World Vision to share slides of a community school that has one book for all learners.

Purpose: to engage learners emotionally; to promote a valuing of books, literature and the ability to get lost in storying whenever they choose; to introduce the *so what* possibility of making a difference in others' lives; learners see a slide displaying a schedule which indicates when each class is given access to the one book;

learners see a slide that shares children reading printed material found in the garbage as English books are not readily available and students must use what they can in order to learn to read.

organiser - 6 thinking hat® evaluation within a 6 t-chart organiser

Purpose: to engage learners emotionally; to promote idea generation and the determination of a *so what;* to collect baseline data on the learner's understanding of the issue; to assist learners in recognising that they need to learn more in order to deal successfully with the issue and generate ideas to remedy it.

Note: while all immersion centres are strategically designed and important, it is critical that learners leave the 'immersion' stage with *so what* possibilities for USING their learning to 'make a difference in their life or the lives of others'. Generally there are one or two key centres that guide learners in their *so what* identification.

Immersion ends with the use of the Clark (reflection, refraction, action) tool.

Learners look back to consider what they now know, or what they have learned thus far (reflection)

From this new foundation, learners are directed to think laterally or divergently (refraction)

- Where can this learning take me?
- How can I use this learning to make a difference in my life or the lives of others?

During this phase of the thinking process, a *so what* to the learning is generated. Learners are directed to reference the *so what* section within the synthesis area of *thinkbox*. The 'action' element of the tool directs the learner to do just that ... take action!

So we know about fairytales ...
So we know about authoring and publishing ...
So we know about the structure of books ...
So we know about illustrations ...
So we know that there are kids in Africa who have no books ...

SO WHAT?
How can we USE what we know to MAKE A DIFFERENCE
IN OUR LIVES OR THE LIVES OF OTHERS?

Step 9: Name the unit

The name of the unit is actually irrelevant. This particular unit could be called, 'Fairytales', it could be called, 'Making a Difference to Children in Africa', or 'Making Books'. It is cross-curricular in its knowledge, process and skill outcomes and as a result could be titled according to many different disciplines. What is important is not the name of the unit but instead the 'endcome' of the unit. All too often the teacher begins the planning process by naming a unit. This can potentially limit the *so what* possibilities that come to mind and in so doing, limit natural interdisciplinary integration of knowledge, processes and skills.

I recommend that you encourage your learners to name the unit ...

As your learners begin their immersion experience, invite them to consider themselves *so what* detectives. Explain that their main job during this time is to determine a purpose or reason for further learning. Once a *so what* has been identified, invite them to name the unit in accordance with the difference they intend to make.

Planning in summary

Plan, plan, plan! Comprehensive planning during the strategic planning phase of *think!nQ* will result in a smooth and effortless inquiry implementation. In your early experience with *think!nQ* it is recommended that you stay fairly tight to your plan. Venturing off route could leave both you and your kids 'lost' to the point where you don't meet required outcomes or a *so what* at the conclusion of your journey. All too often I hear stories from teachers who express that they 'did a great job with immersion but did not get past that stage.' Remember, inquiry that does not result in a *so what* amounts to little more than a research project. It may have been fun, it may have been interesting and they may have learned skills ... unless a learner USES his learning ... it was not relevant! As you and your learners become more confident with both the model and its tools, 'detouring' will be natural, purposeful and manageable.

The planning guideline offered within this handbook is meant to 'immerse' you in what is the most fundamental aspect of *think!nQ* inquiry learning. As you develop your understanding of *think!nQ* planning, further explore the relationships between planning, the design of organisers, frameworks, planners and criteria, your ability to redesign the way in which you see curriculum and deliver it will develop naturally. The 'real thinking' workshop provides a hands-on practical experience to build upon your developing knowledge base. For further information on workshop opportunities, contact office@laneclark.ca

Putting it all together

I have included a step by step guide to using the *thinkbox/thinktower* framework within the *Clark think!nQ real learning process.* You will find the guide on the CD accompanying this book. A sample unit has been provided at both junior and senior levels to demonstrate how the model can be modified to meet individual learner needs. All associated templates (organisers, planners, criteria and frameworks) have been included for your use with students, at both levels. It will correspond directly with this elaborated planning guide.

Specifically, you will find a detailed description of each step of the *!nQuiry*, followed by an outline of the associated types of thinking and all thinking tools and strategies. Each thinking tool can be referenced directly via the hyperlinks which have been built into the design guide. Each thinking tool has been 'tiled' so that you will first find the junior version, immediately followed by the senior version. The seamless infusion of thinking tools and skills into the learning process should become apparent as you read through the *!nQuiry* plan. Upon the completion of each stage of the *think!nQ* framework, it is recommended that you explicitly identify the thinking types, skills and tools used by underlining (or 'dotting') the applicable areas on your 'poster-sized' *thinkbox/thinktower* classroom model. A 'teacher tracking example' has been included to assist you in accurately identifying the thinking types, skills and tools with your learners as they 'track' their thinking (see CD/pg 19). Learners should be encouraged to use a personal black and white *thinkbox* or *thinktower* framework to track their thinking in conjunction with teacher modelling. This has also been included within the CD samples.

A section within the CD organiser has also been provided to enable you to document the specific curriculum learning outcomes or standards associated with each aspect of the learning opportunity.

It is my sincere hope that you found this book and CD both practical and usable! If you take the time to read each page and focus on the tools, strategies and processes provided, I am sure that you will see many opportunities for transfer.

While it is certainly ideal to eventually introduce your learners to thinking and learning through experiences with the entire *think!nQ* approach, it is not a mandatory starting point. Should you feel more confident and comfortable beginning your journey by using one or two tools with your students, you may select individual organisers, frameworks, planners or criteria samples for use within the context of your current teaching practice.

Additional tools can be accessed digitally by registering on the 'get connected' section of www.laneclark.ca. Within the site you will find a wide variety of *thinkchart* organisers, planner's frameworks and criteria. These tools may be substituted for similar tools used within the *Petite!nQuiry* provided on the CD which accompanies this book. They can be used to create a new *!nQuiry* focus; or be used individually within the context of your current practice. The samples provided reflect a diversity of year and developmental levels as well as different curriculum areas. I am adding to the database regularly, as are your colleagues, so log on often!

A workshop setting provides you with the opportunity to experience the approach shared within the pages of this book. The laneclark workshop series offers a developmental approach to professional learning. Each of the eight workshops build on each other. Because learning is developmental for all learners, young and 'not so young' alike, this unique delivery enables and empowers participants to grow their capacity to plan, design, implement, assess and evaluate differently. In addition to working directly within your school setting, public workshop sessions are also available internationally. For more information, please visit www.laneclark.ca or contact office@laneclark.ca.

Regardless of your starting point ... just do it! Remember, learning is a journey, not a destination. Begin your journey now!

Closing thoughts

There is no doubt that there are some absolutely brilliant educators out there working with our students - engaging them, challenging them and extending them. But here is the critical question ... what would the learning look like and sound like if that magical teacher were not in the room, directing the thinking, directing the learning, asking the right question at the right time, providing the right tool at the right time? Designing and delivering through the Clark real thinking process and real learning process is about engagement, enablement and empowerment. It is about the learner owning his thinking and learning. It is about student-directed learning that promotes the development of deep knowledge and understanding while maintaining rigour and curriculum mandates. It is about teaching learners how to think and how to learn. It is about preparing learners for their future, not our past.

Action

1. Read the thinking and learning continuum provided at the back of the book.

2. Plot yourself on the continuum in relation to where you believe your practice is best represented.

3. Move along the continuum in accordance with your starting place. Set realistic goals. Monitor your goals against evidence. Move yourself along the continuum upon the successful achievement of each milestone.

Extended Challenge

1. Read the model unit provided on the CD-ROM resource accompanying this book.

2. Follow the step-by-step guide provided to implement the unit as it has been designed. You can explain to your learners that this opportunity has nothing to do with fairytales; instead it is offering them an opportunity to learn in a different way. Should they enjoy their experience, you will work toward designing and delivering curriculum differently. If you would prefer, you can engage your learners in an alternative inquiry quite easily by substituting the *thinkcharts* along with the inquiry focus.

a glossary of tools to direct thinking

Glossary of Tools

On the following pages you will find a Glossary that refers to a number of tools identified within the pages of this text. Many of these tools can be found, as A4 digital samples, within the CDROM provided at the back of the book. A general description of the main tool categories has been offered below but an in-depth description of each tool has not been provided. Should you be interested in a more detailed outline of these tools, please refer to, *Where Thinking and Learning Meet: Tools to Promote Thinking and Learning*, Lane Clark (Hawler Brownlow Education, 2009)

Frameworks

Frameworks or processes are complex and comprehensive in their design. They outline 'stages' or 'steps' and can incorporate a number of additional thinking tools within their design. Frameworks provide the learner with a picture of the 'whole' while enabling them to focus their attention on the 'parts'. Confusion and incomplete thinking and learning is avoided; self-direction and autonomy are promoted.

Frameworks also promote integration, as all frameworks can be used cross-curricularly. Although a specific framework may be traditionally associated with a particular subject discipline, once understood with a degree of depth and breadth learners eventually select these frameworks in accordance to their 'learning job' only. For example, the 'publisher's cycle' has its origin in the English document of curriculum internationally. It is regularly used to assist learners in their publishing of expository or fictional text. Recognising this, it is its learning job that is key here. A 'Publisher's Process' promotes quality publishing. The discipline is irrelevant. If a learner is 'publishing' a dance in Physical Education, for an audience, then use of the process will assist the learner in this end goal. If a learner is required to 'publish' a website, a report in science, a song in music ... the 'Publisher's Process' should be selected as the tool to promote quality publishing.

Organisers

Learners today have instant access to more information than their ancestors had in a lifetime. A critical aspect of information access is the ability to distinguish between the relevant and irrelevant. Use of a labelled organiser directs the learner and promotes focus on pertinent information only. Further to this, organised information facilitates thinking. With all information readily available in one location, learners are better equipped to analyse and evaluate new information during and following their investigations.

Organisers, framed strategically, also have the capability to direct a learner's processing. An organiser is not an organiser, is not an organiser! All information organisers will direct learners to analyse (examine) and evaluate (make decisions) through the simple act of classification and information management inherent in the design. However, an organiser can be manipulated in its design to heighten, or deepen, the analysis and evaluation that the learner must engage in as they complete the organiser. A learner can also be directed to engage in synthesis type thinking through the explicit framing of the tool.

Planners

Effective planning is a life skill and certainly one which is critical for our learners to develop. Unfortunately, this is easier said than done! Planning demands the consideration of time-lines; the ability to sequence steps and prioritise; it requires the ability to know where you are, where you need to go and how you can get there; a truly powerful plan reflects the desired ends. Given the complexity and abstraction involved in this thinking operation, it is no wonder our learners struggle. Still, the power of a well developed and executed plan cannot be over emphasised - how can we promote and support the development of this critical thinking skill?

Like the organiser tool identified earlier, planners are strategically framed. A well designed planner explicitly details the key elements required to successfully implement or produce something in the future. The greater the understanding of the 'end', the greater the opportunity to develop a truly powerful planner. In essence, the 'criteria for success' is built into the design of this thinking tool.

Evaluation Tools

Decision-making; self assessment, outside assessment, judgment, goal setting, ranking, weighing the value of one idea versus another ... these are some of the skill sets which require evaluative thinking. These are critical skills. These are life skills.

They are certainly skills that we aspire for our learners to develop. Tools can be provided to promote the development of these skill sets.

appendix two:
frameworks

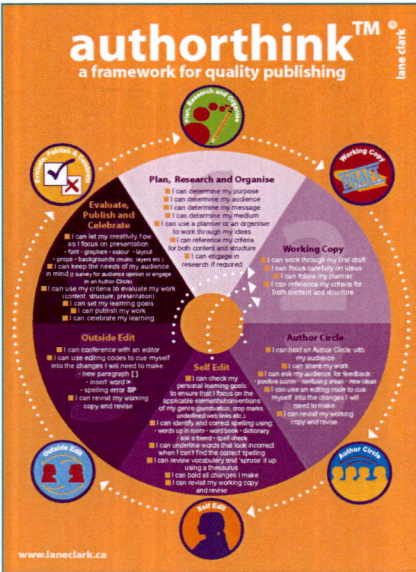

authorthink
a framework for quality publishing

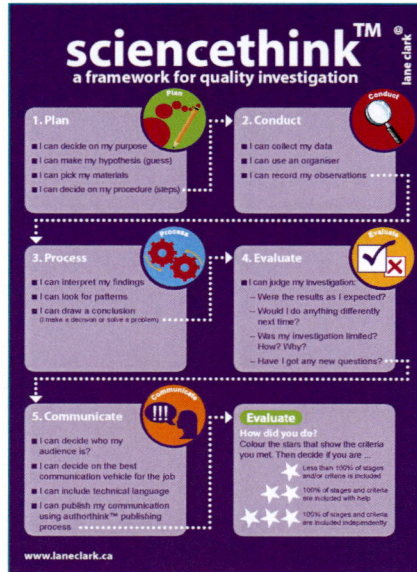

sciencethink
a framework for quality investigations

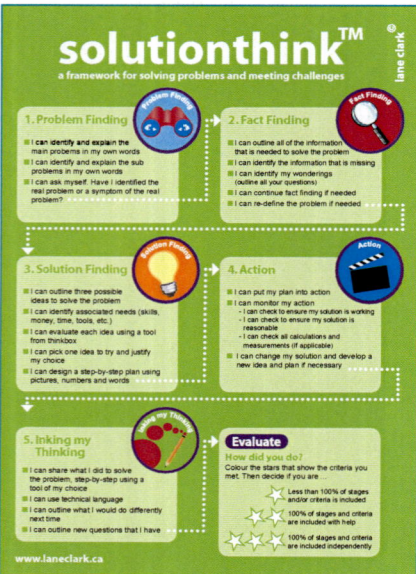

solutionthink
a framework for solving problems or meeting challenges

techthink
a framework for quality producing

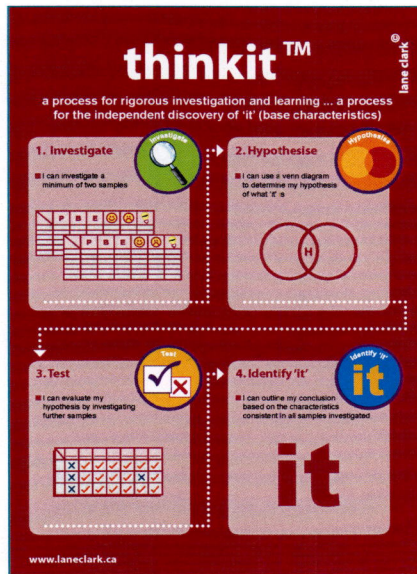

thinkit
a framework for discovering what 'it' is (a fairytale, a fraction, an ecosystem, a sculpture, classical music, basketball - literally anything)

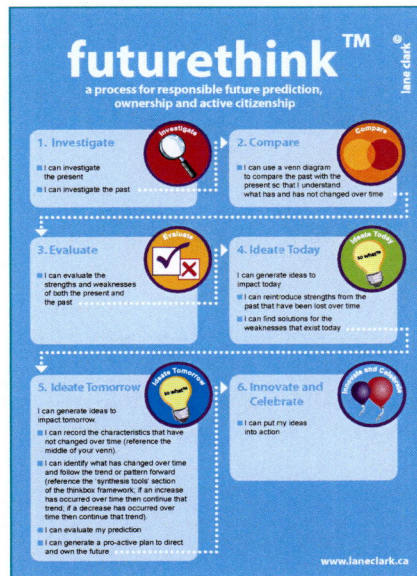

futurethink
a process for responsible future prediction, ownership and active citizenship

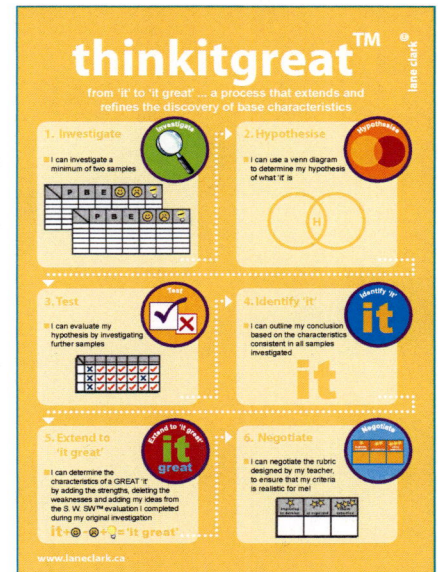

thinkitgreat process
a framework for determining 'GREAT' characteristics (not just the elements of 'it' ... but a 'GREAT' one)

Note: Everything can not be taken to the 'GREAT' stage. For instance what is a GREAT fraction? Learners will therefore only use the process to the 'it' stage.

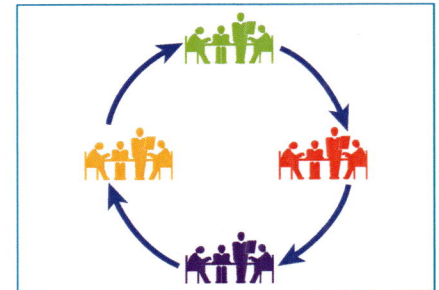

carousel
a co-operative learning framework which promotes group management; learners rotate from one centre to another; the learning at each centre is eventually experienced by all groups of learners

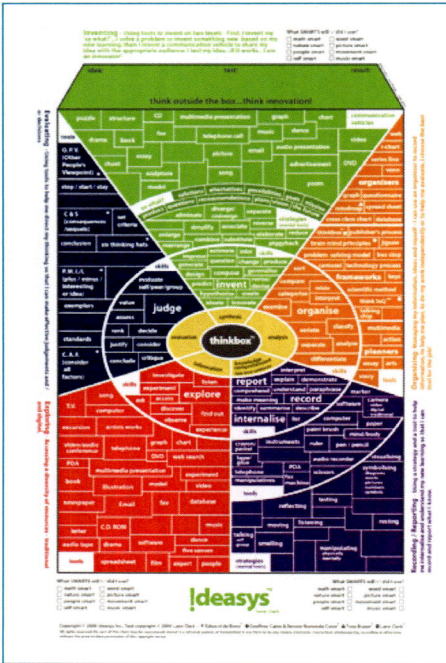

thinkbox

a framework for teaching learners how to think; learners eventually use the model to plan their thinking skills and tools at the beginning of an inquiry; they use the framework to track or identify the thinking skills and tools they actually used during the inquiry - the framework provides 'proof' of thinking

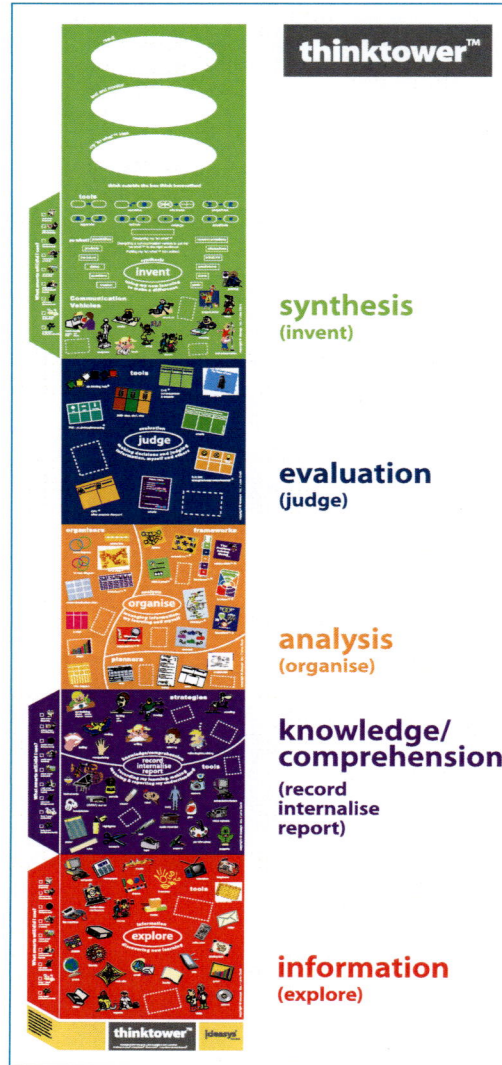

thinktower™

synthesis
(invent)

evaluation
(judge)

analysis
(organise)

knowledge/ comprehension
(record internalise report)

information
(explore)

thinktower

a pictorial framework as per the *thinkbox*; used with visual learners or non-readers

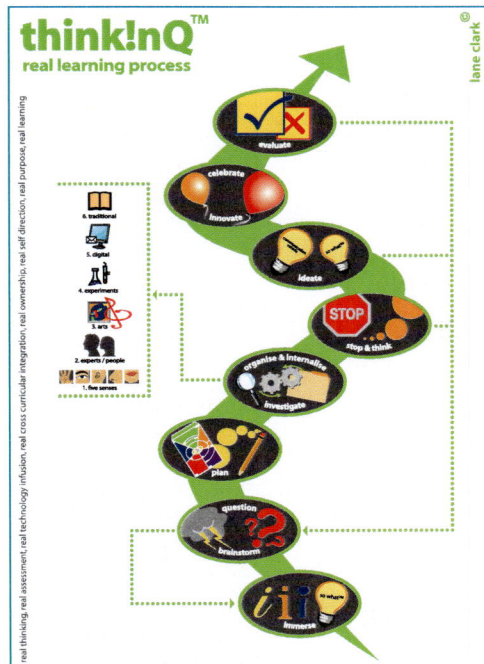

think!nQ (think !nQuiry)

a framework for teaching learners HOW TO LEARN. Learning process is bigger than inquiry. While the inquiry process is embedded in *think!nQ* it remains only a part of the bigger model. *Think!nQ* represents the reverse engineering of how people learn. Use of the model enables learners to independently learn anything. The what is second to the how.

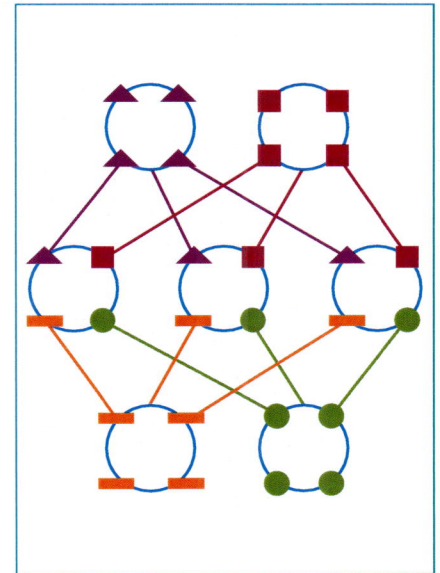

jigsaw

a co-operative learning framework which promotes group management, independence for interdependence, responsibility; a number of home groups are established; each member of each home group is made responsible for becoming an expert in a specific area of focus; experts leave the home team to investigate their specific area of study; each expert returns to the home team to share their area of expertise. All learners are exposed to all areas of focus.

appendix two: organisers

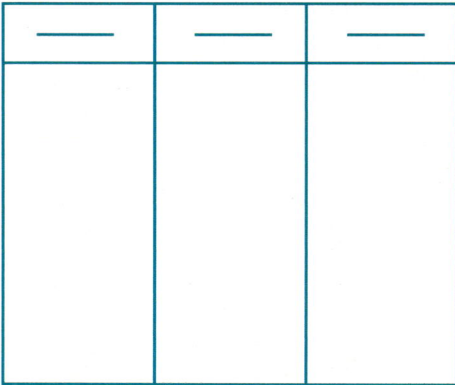

t- chart

an organiser that directs the learner to identify newly acquired information

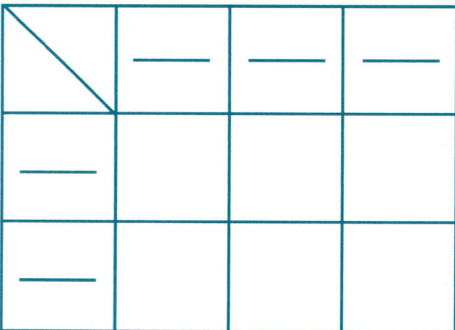

cross classification chart

(also known as a matrix) is an organiser that directs the learner to identify and relate newly acquired information

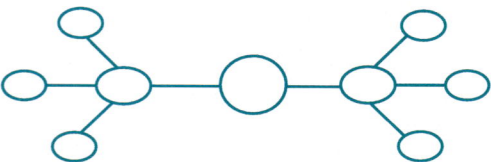

web

an organiser that explicitly encourages the learner to organise from the general to the specific

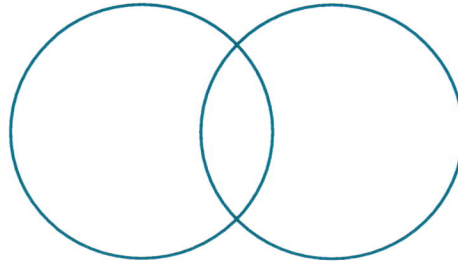

venn diagram

an organiser that explicitly directs the learner to compare and contrast

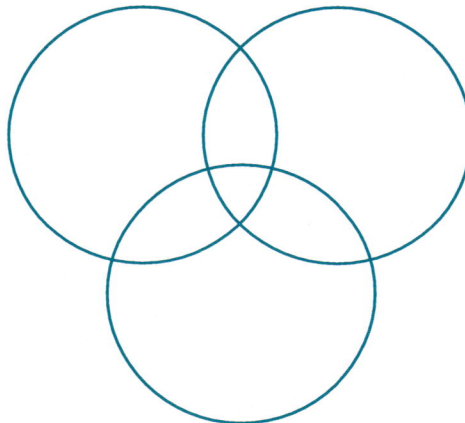

tri-venn diagram

an organiser that explicitly directs the learner to compare and contrast to a more sophisticated level than the venn diagram

series line

an organiser that promotes sequential identification of information

mind map®

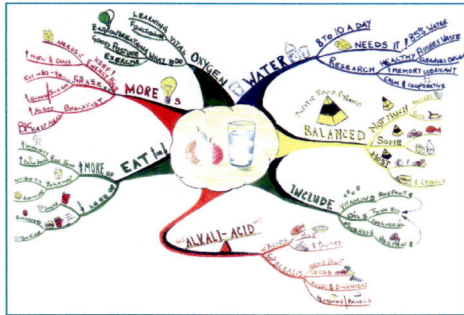

an organiser that promotes long-term memory retention by mirroring the way memories are stored and retrieved in the brain

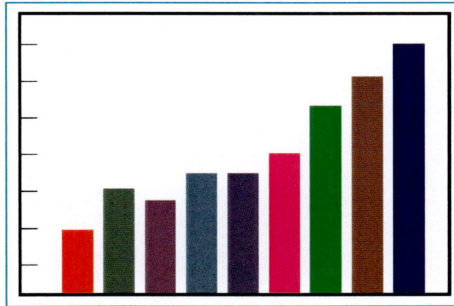

thinkchart

an organiser that embeds rigour and directs processing 'one layer deep'; it promotes cognitive and emotional engagement and explicitly directs the learner to *so what* possibilities

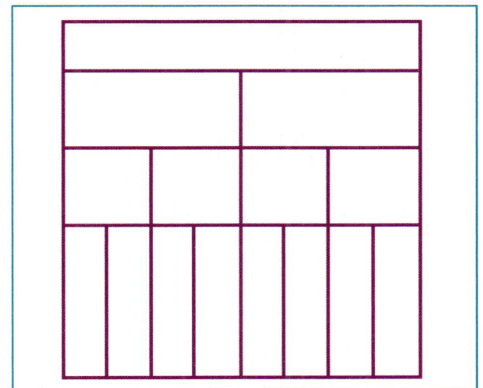

graph

an organiser that explicitly directs the learner toward the representation of relational data

tree diagram

an organiser that explicitly directs the learner to organise information from the general to the specific

spreadsheet

an organiser that promotes the efficient manipulation of data

appendix three:
planners

essay planner

a planner to assist learners in developing an essay; the criteria for the structure of an essay is built into the design of the planner

sciencethink planner

a planner that corresponds to the *sciencethink* framework for quality investigations; use of the planner ensures that all stages of the framework have been explicitly addressed

arts planner

a planner to assist learners in creating an illustration using the principles and elements of design

story planner

a planner to assist learners in developing a story; each specific genre will have its own unique criteria and must therefore be associated with its own planner

video planner

a planner to assist learners in designing a video

appendix four:
evaluation tools

de Bono Tools

Edward de Bono, the leading pioneer in the area of thinking, advocates that thinking requires direction. He believes that thinking can be taught, explicitly, through the use of 'attention directing tools'. De Bono has developed a vast array of tools which direct thinking. Some of his most well known tools direct the development of evaluative thinking and are outlined below for your reference. For further information on de Bono resources, access his website at http://www.edwdebono.com. Please refer to the bibliography for a list of recommended book titles.

PMI (plus, minus and interesting)
Note: interesting is neither good or bad but rather hmmmm (things that make you go hmmmm)

C & S (consequence and sequel)
- immediate, short term, medium term, long term consequences

AGO (aims, goals, objectives)
- do not make a distinction between the three - in general what do we want to end up with/ achieve?

FIP (first important priorities)
- do not worry about 'first' priority - in general what are our priorities?
- a decision cannot be made without acknowledgment of our priorities

OPV (other people's views)
- who is affected by this thinking/action?
- what are the views of those affected?

6 Hats® (each colour symbolically directs thinking from a different perspective)
- colourless (neutral - facts, figures, objective information and questions)
- red (colour of the heart - feelings and intuition)
- yellow (shining sun - benefits/plausible/workable/feasible - logical positive)
- black (storm looming - caution/danger/not plausible - logical negative)
- green (springtime, growth - creative, generative, new ideas, solutions, provocations, alternatives - ideas can be lateral or counter black hat)
- blue (blue sky above all else - looking down at thinking - overview - where are we, next steps, summary, observations, checker of bias, control of other hats and thinking steps)

There are a number of tools, in addition to those created by de Bono, that appear in the 'evaluation' section of your *thinkbox* model. These can be found over the page.

The *S.W.SW* (strengths, weakness, *so what* idea)

This tool is similar to the PMI tool developed by de Bono; however it stretches the learner further in their thinking and must not be used interchangeably. When using this tool, learners consider the strengths (like the positives) and the weaknesses (like the minuses). At this point, the similarities between these two tools ends. The final SW directs the learner to consider a *so what* idea to move beyond considering that which is 'interesting' to the generation of a way forward. The *so what* corresponds to *thinkbox* where learners are invited to consider: recommendations, alternatives, goals, solutions, new products that can be created. The *S.W.SW* tool promotes analytical, evaluative and synthesis types of thinking.

RRA (reflection, refraction, action)

Reflection, refraction, action can be used in conjunction with the SWSW tool or independently.

Reflection: Learners look back to consider what they now know, or what they have learned thus far

Refraction: From this new foundation, learners are directed to think laterally or divergently

- Where can this learning take me?
- How can I use this learning to make a difference in my life or the lives of others?

At this time, learners determine a *so what* idea.

Action: The learner is directed to act on their *so what* idea. All too often, great ideas are left untried. Learners are invited to act on their new ideas. If learners are using either the *thinkbox* or *thinktower* frameworks, they would be encouraged to monitor the implementation or 'action' and record the outcome.

V & SB (values and supporting beliefs)

value: that which is held as important

belief: something which is held as true

This tool directs the learner to consider their values prior to making a decision or generating new ideas. All too often thinking decisions are made independent of the explicit consideration of values. When using this tool, learners are directed to consider their values in a diversity of areas (family, environment, friendships etc.) prior to making a final decision. A learner's ability to describe what a value 'looks like' or 'sounds like' ensures that the value is truly understood and not simply espoused. Including values and supporting beliefs in one's criteria for decision-making and idea generation will promote the development of 'ethical' thinking - certainly something worth aspiring toward! (i.e. I value the environment. As a result, I believe it is wrong to use containers that cannot be recycled in our celebration of learning.)

Stop, Start, Stay

This tool directs the user to reflect back on a situation, an idea, a behaviour, a specific piece of work, a product, or a process engaged in.

What hasn't worked? What needs to be stopped?

What is going well? What has worked? What needs to stay?

What needs to be done differently? What is missing? What do I need to start?

Criteria

The definition of criteria is simple: a standard of judgment; a rule. Criteria for the learner is just that ... his judging rules.

Criteria sets the learner up for success. It enables a learner to know where they are, where they are going and how they will get there. Unfortunately, most exemplars of criteria fall short of really enabling and empowering a learner to achieve this. If criteria is truly going to work for our learners and teachers, it must be developed using the *Clark criteria for criteria.*

It must be developed in kid speak. If a learner cannot use the criteria independently, we've completely defeated the purpose of the tool. It must be specific both in terms of quantity and quality. Failure to do this will result in a need for moderation. It is critical that we recognise that moderation is a symptom of a grand fundamental problem ... subjective criteria!

While it is relatively simple to specify quantity, the only way to specify quality is to embed thinking into the design of the criteria. Criteria must be observable and measurable. This means that a learner and teacher must assess and evaluate against evidence. At no point in time should a learner or teacher be evaluating based on what they 'remember' or what they recorded in 'anecdotals'. I can tell a learner that they didn't stop at a full stop; that they didn't raise their voice for the question mark; OR they can listen to the audio recording themselves and reference their criteria to determine for themselves their own strengths and needs. Which approach will be more effective for the learner? Finally, criteria must be realistic for the learner who is using it. You can provide a learner with the most wonderful criteria ... it is written in kid speak; it is specific; measurable and observable. When the learner uses it, they find themselves unsuccessful. It must be more than wonderful criteria; it must be wonderful for the learner using it! We know that success breeds success. When using assessment criteria, nothing is more critical than our learners meeting with success. The right criteria for the learner will promote this. While you may at this point have visions of 32 students and 32 different pieces of criteria - this will not be the case. It is both an art and a science to create truly effective criteria. For a complete guide to the *Clark criteria for criteria,* see *where thinking, learning and assessment meet,* Clark (Hawker Brownlow Education, 2009).

frequently asked and frequently not asked questions

How long does it take learners before they can own the *think!nQ* learning process and design their own inquiries?

Independence is conditional of many factors which include age, developmental leveland experience with frameworks for thinking and learning. However, independence can be promoted by ensuring that the teacher, while modeling the process, makes every aspect of the thinking and learning transparent to the learner in the following ways:

Thinking Tools

Name each thinking tool that you have planned into the inquiry when it's introduced, and explicitly highlight each tool, as it's used, on your classroom sized model of *thinkbox* or *thinktower*. Learners will learn the names of the thinking tools and, as importantly, begin to learn which thinking tools are used at specific points during the learning process. **Understanding the relationship between thinking tool use and the stages of the learning process is critical if the learner is ever going to independently direct their own inquiries and be able to self-select the right thinking tools at the right time during their learning journey.**

Tracking Thinking

Provide learners with their own black and white copy of the *thinkbox* or *thinktower* thinking frameworks; and encourage them to identify and underline the thinking tools that they used over the course of their *think!nQ* inquiry upon its conclusion. **Learners must know the names of the thinking tools planned and implemented by the teacher if they are to one day independently plan and implement these tools themselves.**

The *think!nQ Real Learning Process*

Ensure that you provide learners with the black and white student model of the *think!nQ learning process*; and encourage learners to colour in or highlight each stage as it's completed. **Learners must know the name of each stage and the correct order if they are to plan and implement their own inquiries one day.**

Evaluate Thinking and Learning

Upon the conclusion of the inquiry, ensure that learners reflect upon and evaluate the thinking tools that were used throughout the course of the inquiry as well as their experience at each stage of the *think!nQ learning process*. The *S.W.SW* tool can be used to encourage learners to consider the strengths and weaknesses of the thinking tools used and learning process stages experienced. The final SW will direct learners to consider *so what* ideas for:

- improving their use of specific thinking tools
- trying thinking tools not yet introduced
- omitting specific tools that weren't effective for them
- improving their ability to navigate through specific stages of the learning process
- altering specific learning experiences planned by the teacher at specific stages of the learning process

When a learner can analyse and evaluate what the teacher has planned and implemented; and suggest changes for improvement, they are proving a depth and breadth of knowledge and understanding which will enable them to responsibly and rigorously begin to take ownership of their thinking and learning.

At this time, collaborative planning of the learning process, and the thinking tools to be used therein, should occur. Continued transparency will result in the learner's ability to engage in independent, self-directed autonomous use of the *think!nQ learning process* and the *thinkbox/thinktower* thinking frameworks.

Consistency

Ensure that you are consistently using the *think!nQ learning process*, and the *thinkbox* and *thinktower* thinking frameworks, to design and deliver learning opportunities for your learners. If the use of the approach, tools, strategies, processes, models and language is haphazard, learners won't have the opportunity to internalise the knowledge and skills required to one day 'own' their thinking and learning. **Consistent use will assist both the learner and teacher in developing confidence and competence.**

Do the kids ever get tired of filling in organisers?

If an organiser has been strategically framed to promote the attainment of specific knowledge, and promote the learner's processing of that knowledge, the learner will appreciate the way in which the tool facilitates their thinking and learning. Because the graphic organiser is designed for succinct, sharp recordings, even the reluctant writer is more likely to experience success when recording and internalising accessed data. Non-writers can effectively use self-made or commercial pictures, symbols and/or photographs when recording on graphic organisers; by providing the learner with an information organiser on a computer, audio recordings can be used instead of written text when completing the organiser.

In order to maintain freshness, teachers should also consider altering the learner's level of independent use of graphic organisers. The teacher can complete the organiser in a 'whole class' experience; alternatively, interpersonal skills can be promoted by providing one large organiser to a group of students to complete as a team. By including the initials of an individual beside their contribution, accountability can be promoted and monitored.

Aren't all inquiry frameworks the same?

The promotion of inquiry-based instruction is certainly on the rise. But beware, all inquiry models are not the same! Unfortunately, most inquiry models amount to little more than glorified research frameworks. The teacher attempts to capture the learner's interest; the learner is then invited to develop their own questions; they are then encouraged to conduct research in search of answers to their questions; the learner is then directed to share their findings with their classmates; finally they are invited to evaluate their learning and set goals. On the surface, this sounds effective enough but upon closer reflection and examination ... is it really?

In 'real' world learning, you have a purpose *before* you engage further in the learning process. Your purpose drives your need to ask questions; it drives your need for knowledge and your need for skills; it motivates you and of course interests you. It's your reason for demonstrating persistence, checking for accuracy, thinking about your thinking, applying past knowledge (Art Costa's Habits of Mind). *The Clark think!nQ real learning process* recognises and strategically mirrors this reality during the 'immersion' stage. Learners do not leave this stage of the model prior to identifying their *so what* purpose.

When engaged in 'real' learning outside of the school walls, you don't develop arbitrary questions to research because you are told to. In the *think!nQ* framework, learners develop strategic questions which are required in order to meet their *so what* challenge; at the planning stage the learner is provided with a thinking framework to assist them in self-selecting the thinking tools needed to direct their thinking and promote their learning; their research is purposeful. They are not researching mindlessly because they happen to be at that particular stage of the model. In the *think!nQ* inquiry framework, the stop and think stage directs the learner to self assess their knowledge, understanding and skills. At this stage, the learner discerns their readiness level to move forward. 'Have I acquired the necessary knowledge, understandings and skills? Do I need to revisit the investigation stage?' This is a critical stage in the real learning process and seldom included in most inquiry models.

In 'real' world learning, the learner does not research for the sole purpose of telling their friends what they found out upon the conclusion of their research. Unfortunately, this is the case in far too many inquiry models offered to schools, promoted in books or by consultants. In the *Clark think!nQ real learning process*, once the learner has acquired the necessary knowledge, understandings and skills, they USE their learning to make a difference in their life and the lives of others. The learner identified their *so what* or purpose prior to leaving the immersion stage; then at the ideate stage, the learner develops and refines the *so what* idea that drove the entire inquiry. The learner acts on their new learning to solve problems that they have become aware of; to develop alternatives, recommendations, new possibilities; to design and develop new products, etc.

Rather than communicating what they learned to their 'friends', the learner is directed to consider the authentic audience for their *so what* idea. Who needs to receive their recommendations? Who have they developed the product for? Who was the solution developed for? What is the best communication vehicle given that message and that specific audience? Contrary to what occurs at the communication or sharing stage of most inquiry models, the *think!nQ real learning process* directs the learner to develop authentic communication vehicles for authentic audiences.

When engaged in 'real' world learning, an effective learner evaluates their learning. While I recognise that this stage is often included in many other inquiry models, it is significantly extended within the *Clark think!nQ* inquiry framework.

First, the learner puts their *so what* into action during the innovate stage of the model; they are also directed to test and monitor the success of that implementation.

Did the solution work?

Did the recommendations or alternatives make a difference?

Did the product work?

By evaluating the success of the *so what* idea, the learner's ability to design ideas and innovate are promoted and developed. Because these results often take time, students live the reality that the learning isn't complete simply because the term is over.

The learner's ability to engage in rigorous evaluation is also encouraged during the evaluate stage of the *think!nQ real learning process*, as learners explicitly identify the thinking tools used on their *thinkbox* or *thinktower*; consider the strengths and weaknesses of both their thinking and learning, and outline goals to improve in both their thinking and learning.

The celebrate stage of the *Clark think!nQ* framework represents another stage that is seldom, if ever, included in other inquiry models. In addition to validating the learning and valuing the work and effort engaged in by the learner, this stage of the Clark model of inquiry enables learners to engage in a wide range of authentic opportunities. For example: planning menus, working within budgets; cooking for large numbers; following, converting, extending recipes; developing and working within timelines; organising spaces; learning the skills of a host/hostess; creating and sending invitations; etc.

How will I assess and evaluate my learners if they learn in this way?

The *think!nQ real learning process* is founded on the user's curriculum documents. Many inquiry approaches also offer the user guidance in regard to planning but often invite them to 'back map' the curriculum after determining a topic, theme or issue. This can be problematic for the teacher who is accountable to specific learning outcomes.

Learning is developmental and a learner can only build upon the foundation of knowledge, understanding and skills that they possess. I believe that teachers talk this talk but often act outside of this research in regard to curriculum and instructional design. As discussed in Section 2, Chapter 1, Thinking About Thinking, if we want our learners to develop deep knowledge and deep understanding we must respect the manner in which this is achieved. If we want our learners to use their knowledge about biomes to design recommendations to improve problems identified within a biome, they must first have depth of knowledge and understanding in the area of ecosystems; depth and breadth of knowledge and understanding in regard to ecosystems would require prerequisite knowledge and understanding of plant and animal adaptation; this would require foundational knowledge in the area of plant and animal life cycles; which necessitates knowledge and understanding of the characteristics of plants and animals; which in turn requires knowledge and understanding of living and non-living things.

While this last example focuses on the developmental nature of content knowledge, little changes when dealing with process or skill development. For example, if a learner wanted to share recommendations through a persuasive piece written for the local newspaper, the learner would need to demonstrate skill sets in paragraph writing; they would need skills in composing an introduction, body and conclusion; this would require skill in their ability to develop a topic sentence and closing sentence; which would require skill in writing a diversity of sentences. Of course I could continue this pattern, but what is important is the recognition that all learning is developmental and requires prerequisites if quality, depth and breadth are sought-after aspects of learning.

By 'back mapping' curriculum to fit into a theme, topic or issue, the curriculum that doesn't 'fit' is often forced, addressed superficially or omitted altogether. Subsequently, mandated outcomes cannot be accurately assessed, and more importantly, prerequisite knowledge for later learning is often not attained or only attained at a superficial level that precludes the learner's ability to build on it.

The *Clark 9 step planning process* guides the user in their ability to develop a comprehensive *think!nQ* inquiry, as well as ensuring the integration of curriculum knowledge, skills and process outcomes.

By beginning with the content or knowledge outcomes of a curriculum document, the developer of the inquiry explicitly embeds developmentally sequenced, mandated outcomes within the design of the inquiry. Because these outcomes are 'unpacked' in great detail and then embedded within the framing of organisers, knowledge acquisition is proven as the learner completes their organisers. Critically, the *so what* represents how a learner will use their new knowledge to make a difference in their life and the lives of others. Performance based assessment and evaluation becomes a reality when the learner acts on their *so what* during the ideate stage. If a learner can USE their new knowledge, outcomes are proven at a sophisticated level that is superior to simply identifying new knowledge through test questions or a PowerPoint presentation.

At stage 6 of the Planning Process, cross-curricular processes are planned into the inquiry along with associated criteria; and at stage 7, cross-curricular skills are embedded and associated criteria explicitly developed. In the *Clark 9 step inquiry planning process*, knowledge, process and skill outcomes are designed purposefully and strategically into the inquiry; and criteria is developed so that all outcomes are explicit for both the teacher and the learners. Explicit criteria enables and empowers the learner to self assess so that they are responsible for proving outcomes. Of course, if the criteria works for the learner, it will also work for the teacher!

How is personalised learning addressed through this approach?

Learners enter into new learning and thinking opportunities with very different background knowledge, skills and abilities. Acknowledging that we can only build upon the foundation that a learner has is one of the critical realisations that we can make as educators.

A teacher can design magical learning opportunities for their learners. Knowledge, skills and processes can be firmly embedded in experiences that are engaging and authentic. But if the knowledge, processes and/or skills are beyond the ability level of the learner, the magic won't ever be realised. Conversely, if the knowledge, process and/or skills are below the learner, boredom will set in and the learner will be 'switched off' to the possibility of the magic. Developing learning opportunities that are 'right' for each learner is the challenge. Anything short of this will result in lost achievement.

In the Clark approach to thinking and learning, criteria for knowledge, skills and processes is embedded into the design of all learning; and each is formatted as a continuum. The learner is empowered to place themselves on this continuum using baseline data as a reference. The learner may then move themselves forward on the continuum should the learning prove too easy, or back should the learning prove too difficult. The teacher is taught to conduct 'clinics' or 'target teaching opportunities' for learners in reference to specific areas on the continua.

Students are 'target taught' in homogeneous groups that focus strategically on the specific needs of those learners working on the designated skills, process and/or knowledge of the continua. While this learning occurs in homogeneous groups these groups are 'fluid' on a 'moment to moment' basis. Should a learner meet the criteria outlined in the area of the continua they are focused on, and can prove this attainment against evidence, they can move themselves on.

How is inclusive learning addressed within this approach?

Successful learning requires input, processing and output. In order for a learner to do their very best learning, they must access information using modalities of strength and they must be provided with opportunities to process or internalise the new information using modalities of strength. Finally, when the learner communicates what they have learned, they again use a modality of strength. Only then will they truly be enabled to share what they know.

Generally in the design and delivery of curriculum the teacher often mandates the ways in which a learner finds out (input). Moreover explicit internalisation time (processing) is rarely designed into the learning opportunity, and the final means of communicating what the learner knows is also mandated by the teacher. I believe that this approach is having significantly detrimental effects on the achievement of learning outcomes.

In the Clark approach to thinking and learning, teachers are provided with the knowledge, skills and tools required to engage in MI (Multiple Intelligences) inclusive classroom practice. While it is critical that our students are able to take in, process and express their learning through their modalities of strength, it is by focusing on the weaker modalities and encouraging learners to work on these areas of difficulty that those weaker modalities will be developed. Consequently, an MI inclusive practice ensures that the learner engages all modalities when learning.

In the Lane Clark approach, tools for accessing, internalising and expressing are selected collaboratively with students and cross-checked against all learning modalities. To ensure that all modalities are engaged, learners are responsible to use all identified tools during each stage of their learning and thinking; however, they may sequence their use of these tools so that they focus on areas of strength before areas of weakness. Teacher 'must dos' are embedded into the design of the learning but student 'picks' precede any teacher 'must do' component.

The privilege of power, ownership, control and personalisation are balanced with responsible decision-making.

Isn't it a lot of 'jargon' for kids to learn?

It is critical that students be immersed in the 'language of thinking'; that the teacher speaks the language consistently; and that the learner be expected to use the language when referring to thinking tools, strategies and processes. I expect my learners to speak the 'language of maths or science' and I expect them to speak the 'language of thinking'. We don't consider the terms observation, hypothesis or conclusion to be jargon within the science discipline; we don't consider the terms narrator, genre and thesis jargon within English; nor do we suggest the terms sum, hypotenuse and numerator to be jargon in maths. This vocabulary, quite simply, represents the technical language of the discipline. The technical language of thinking includes terms such as: *think!nQ* inquiry, ideate, brainstorm, *S.W.SW*, *authorthink*, *sciencethink* and *techthink*, analyse, evaluate, synthesise, venn diagram, cross classification chart, the 6 Thinking Hats, and so on.

Without a shared language, it will be impossible for you and your students to develop a thinking culture, as language is a critical component of culture. It is required if you and learners wish to engage in substantive conversations about thinking; and it is paramount to the learner's ability to one day self-select their thinking tools and engage in the learning process independently.

bibliography

Barth, Roland. *Improving Schools from Within.* San Francisco: Jossey-Bass Publishers, 1990.

Bennett, Barrie, Carol Rolheiser-Bennett and Laurie Stevahn. *Where Heart Meets Mind.* Toronto: Educational Connections, 1991.

Buzan, Tony and Barry Buzan. *The Mind Map Book.* London: BBC Books, 1995.

Buzan, Tony. *Head Strong.* London: Harper Collins Publishers, 2001.

Caine, Geoffery, Renata, Caine & Sam Crowell. *Mindshifts.* Tuscan, AZ: Zephyr Press, 1999.

Caine, Geoffery and Renata Caine. *Unleashing the Power of Perceptual Change: The potential of brain based teaching.* Alexandria, VA: ASCD, 1997.

Carter, Rita. *Mapping the Mind.* London: Phoenix, 2000.

Covey, Stephen. *The Seven Habits of Highly Effective People.* New York: Simon and Schuster, 1989.

Covey, Stephen. *The 8th Habit.* New York: Simon and Schuster, 2005

de Bono, Edward. *Parallel Thinking.* England: Penguin Books, 1995.

de Bono, Edward. *Six Thinking Hats.* Boston: Little Brown and Company, 1995.

de Bono, Edward. *Thinking Course.* London: BBC Worldwide Ltd., re-issued 2004.

Diamond, Marian and Janet Hopson. *Magic Trees of the Mind.* England: Penguin Books, 1999.

Dryden, Gordon and Jeannette Vos. *The Learning Revolution.* New Zealand: The Learning Web, 1997.

Friedman, Thomas. *The Lexus and the Olive Tree.* London: Harper Collins Publishers, 1999.

Friedman, Thomas. *The World is Flat.* Australia: Penguin Group, 2006.

Fullan, Michael. *Change Forces.* London: The Falmer Press, 1993.

Gardner, Howard. *The Disciplined Mind.* New York: Simon & Schuster Inc., 1999.

Gardner, Howard. *Frames of Mind* (Tenth Anniversary Edition). USA: Basic Books, 1993.

Gray, Bob and Adrian Jones. *ChemCert Agvet Chemical Users Course Resource Manual.* (Ninth Edition) Australia: ChemCert Australia, 2005.

Gleick, James. *Chaos.* London: Vintage, 1998.

Grantham, Charles. *The Future of Work.* New York: McGraw-Hill, 2000

Marzano, Robert. *A Different Kind of Classroom: Teaching With Dimensions of Learning.* Melbourne, Vic: Hawker Brownlow Education. 1992, 2006.

Peters, Tom. *The Circle of Innovation.* New York: Knopf Inc., 1997.

Peters Tom. *Re-imagine!* London: Dorling Kindersley Limited, 2003.

Pinker, Steven. *How the Mind Works.* London: Penguin Books,1998.

Senge, Peter. *The Fifth Discipline.* New York: Currency and Doubleday, 1990.

Winston, Robert. *The Human Mind.* London: Bantam Press, 2003.